THE
ENTREPRENEUR
ROLLER COASTER

YOUR ESSENTIAL GUIDE BOOK FOR
THRIVING AS AN ENTREPRENEUR

DARREN HARDY

—*NEW YORK TIMES* BESTSELLING AUTHOR

This publication is designed to provide general information regarding the subject matter covered. However, laws and practices often vary from state to state and are subject to change. Because each factual situation is different, specific advice should be tailored to the particular circumstances. For this reason, the reader is advised to consult with his or her own advisor regarding their specific situation.

The author and publisher have taken reasonable precautions in the preparation of this book and believe the facts presented in the book are accurate as of the date it was written. However, neither the author nor the publisher assumes any responsibility for any errors or omissions. The author and publisher specifically disclaim any liability resulting from the use or application of the information contained in this book, and the information is not intended to serve as legal, financial, or other professional advice related to individual situations.

 Published by REARDEN PRESS
Miami Beach, Florida 33139
ReardenPress.com

©2015 by Darren Hardy

For ordering information or special discounts for bulk purchases, contact DARREN HARDY, LLC at 760.230.4454.

Design and composition by Accelerate Media Partners LLC
Cover design by Kim Baker

Cataloging-in-Publication data

ISBN: 978-1-7335133-0-2

Printed in China

20 21 22 23 24 25   13 12 11 10 9 8 7 6 5 4

PRAISE FOR *THE ENTREPRENEUR ROLLER COASTER*
—WHY NOW IS THE TIME TO *#JOINTHERIDE*

"Darren Hardy does it AGAIN! *The Entrepreneur Roller Coaster* is going to be the must-read book of the year for anyone who runs their own business or wants to. I really wish I had this book 20 years ago when I started my entrepreneur journey; it would have saved me a ton of pain and shortened my learning curve. Now is your time; join the ride!"
—**David Bach,** nine-time *New York Times* best-selling author of *Start Late, Finish Rich* and *The Automatic Millionaire*, founder of FinishRich.com

"Darren Hardy is the real deal! *The Entrepreneur Roller Coaster* is chock-full of smart nuggets you will put to use right away!"
—**Barbara Corcoran,** star of ABC's *Shark Tank* and author of *Shark Tales*

"To win in business you need to be tough, think big, and become skilled. To become the best, you have to train with the best. Darren Hardy lives and breathes success! If you are serious about success, this book will help you get to the top. You're going to love the view."
—**Donald Trump,** chairman and president of The Trump Organization

"There has never been a better time than NOW to become a bold entrepreneur. Darren Hardy hits all the essentials to be a successful entrepreneur that nobody teaches in school—courage, passion, purpose, persistence, bold thinking, and so much more. This book is a must-read before joining the ride of entrepreneurship."
—**Peter H. Diamandis,** CEO of XPRIZE, executive chairman of Singularity University, author of the *New York Times* best-seller *Abundance: The Future Is Better Than You Think*

"Darren Hardy has studied the greats of our time. He's interviewed them, learned from them, and distilled it all into one book. Honestly, how else are you going to get access to the wisdom of some of the greatest business minds in history?"
—**Dave Liniger,** founder and chairman of RE/MAX LLC

"This book is an incredible resource! Not only does it provide the perfect combination of the necessary mind-set and skill sets you need to develop to become a successful entrepreneur, but it is written in such a straightforward yet entertaining way that you can't put it down. Darren's transparency, humor, and no-holds-barred style of writing had me turning page after page to see what was next. Even after 45 years of starting and running several successful businesses, I kept learning something new. Highly recommended."
—**Jack Canfield,** international best-selling author of the *Chicken Soup for the Soul* series and *The Success Principles*

"Darren Hardy is a man on a mission. He's seen a way for you to move forward, and he's generous enough to share it. Listen up!"
—**Seth Godin,** author of *The Icarus Deception*

"Life is a roller coaster, and as Darren says, so is success. He and I both agree that each of us has our own measure of what it means to be successful, and figuring out what it means to you is the work of a lifetime. This book will help you define success on your own terms."
—**Maria Shriver,** six-time *New York Times* best-selling author, Peabody and Emmy Award-winning journalist, *NBC News* special anchor, and former First Lady of California

"The future belongs to entrepreneurs—and Darren's new book is a handbook that would-be entrepreneurs need for starting, growing, and sustaining a successful business in the wild, roller-coaster-ride world of entrepreneurship."
—**Robert Kiyosaki,** educator, entrepreneur, investor and author of *Rich Dad, Poor Dad*

"Success leaves clues. Darren Hardy has not only mastered the Entrepreneur Roller Coaster ride for himself, but he has also interviewed, studied, and spent time with the greatest entrepreneurs alive today. I am calling this the must-read book to be properly onboarded into entrepreneurship. This is your guidebook to unleashing your potential and awakening the entrepreneurial giant, ready and waiting, within you."
—**Anthony Robbins,** chairman to seven privately held companies, *New York Times* best-selling author, and Peak Performance coach

"Rar! My heart rate is racing as I tear through this riveting book. Darren captures and spreads that entrepreneurial spirit better than anyone I know. I've been a successful entrepreneur for 25 years but *The Entrepreneur Roller Coaster* just got me more excited and enlightened than I've been in a long time. You must read and USE this immediately!"
—**Derek Sivers,** founder of CD Baby and author of *Anything You Want*

"The clarity and insight Darren Hardy delivers can help transform a struggling entrepreneur into an incredibly successful one. From prioritizing and delegating to leadership, Hardy delivers some of the best insights out there. Anyone wanting to achieve great success should put *The Entrepreneur Roller Coaster* on their short list of must-read books."
—**John Assaraf,** serial entrepreneur and *New York Times* best-selling author of *Having It All* and *The Answer*

"Darren Hardy's new book *The Entrepreneur Roller Coaster* is a blueprint for aspiring entrepreneurs. He takes you on the ride in the front car, through the peaks and valleys, and all at full speed. Darren's concepts are proven, and his strategies are gold. Buy it and enjoy YOUR success ride."
—**Jeffrey Gitomer,** author of *Little Red Book of Selling*

"If you're going to get on the roller coaster of entrepreneurship, make sure you're in the front seat! You're in for the ride of your life with Darren Hardy's new adventure book for those who dream of having their own business. Get your ticket."
—**Grant Cardone,** *New York Times* best-selling author of *If You're Not First, You're Last*, entrepreneur and founder of Whatever It Takes Network

"This is it! It has taken me 20-plus years to learn what Darren has condensed down into 200-plus pages. Read, study, and devour this book. It will cut down your learning curve, accelerate your success, and change the prosperity of your future."
—**Daymond John,** star of ABC's *Shark Tank* and founder/CEO of FUBU

"If you want to learn how to manage uncertainty in your business and personal life, then you MUST read this book twice. Read it once to gain the skills to survive the ride, and read it a second time to apply the tools Darren gives you to enjoy the thrill of the ride, as it's less scary when you apply your new skills!"
—**Alex Mandossian,** chief engagement officer of MarketingOnline.com

"This book is fuel for your entrepreneurial fire. If you have the desire, this book will provide you with the ideas and motivation essential to striking out and succeeding. Don't wait any longer; read this book and go for your dream."
—**Mark Sanborn,** best-selling author of *The Fred Factor* and *The Encore Effect*

"Darren Hardy is one of the world's preeminent experts on how to get to be great as an entrepreneur. Read this book. Mark it up. Act on it swiftly! And win."
—**Robin Sharma,** best-selling author of *The Leader Who Had No Title*

"This remarkable book is loaded with practical, proven methods and techniques that you can use to save yourself thousands of dollars and years of hard work."
—**Brian Tracy,** author of *The Way to Wealth*

"Now is the best time to become an entrepreneur, and with Darren's new book *The Entrepreneur Roller Coaster*, you'll have a plan for succeeding. Not only are Darren's insights on prioritization, delegation, and leadership great, but you'll also learn what it REALLY takes to build a successful business, overcome obstacles on the path to success, and what the world's top achievers know about making their dreams come true."
—**Joe Polish,** founder of Genius Network

"The clarity and insight Darren Hardy delivers can help transform a struggling entrepreneur into an incredibly successful one."
—**Chip Conley,** Joie de Vivre Hospitality founder and *New York Times* best-selling author of *Emotional Equations* and *Peak*

"*The Entrepreneur Roller Coaster* is a must-read for all smart and ambitious business owners. Darren Hardy is a master at explaining what it really takes to win in modern business (and in life), and this book provides the road map for starting and scaling your dream company successfully. If you want to survive the emotional ride to wealth, then buy this book now."
—**Brendon Burchard,** *New York Times* best-selling author of *The Millionaire Messenger*

"*The Entrepreneur Roller Coaster* can help anyone who has always wanted to be an entrepreneur but never knew where to begin or what to expect."
—**Tony Hsieh,** CEO of Zappos and *New York Times* best-selling author of *Delivering Happiness*

"Darren Hardy's book is brilliant—a masterpiece! This is exactly the right combination of cradling entrepreneurs gently, and then kicking their asses into gear. Plus, the 'insider' stories Darren shares of his interviews with superachievers such as Branson and Jobs kept me riveted. This book is like having private access to some of the greatest entrepreneurial minds of our time."
—**Marc A. Sparks,** founder of Timber Creek Capital and author of *They Can't Eat You*

"If you truly want to build a successful business, and you want to do it without killing yourself in the process, this is the book for you."
—**Nido Qubein,** president of High Point University and chairman of Great Harvest Bread Company

"Every couple of centuries a revolutionary book comes along and transforms the business world forever; *The Entrepreneur Roller Coaster* is such a book. Darren Hardy is the most brilliant mind in business today. I have never read a book that is so compelling, clear, and concise and that holds the key to changing your business and your future. Darren delivers the 'Entrepreneurial Playbook' with unprecedented focus! Enjoy the ride!"
—**Todd Duncan,** *New York Times* best-selling author of *Time Traps and High Trust Selling*

"Darren Hardy has interviewed the most successful entrepreneurs of all time, and turned those insights into a step-by-step guide to help you build an amazing business. Courtesy of this book, there is a road map for you to build a wildly successful business by avoiding critical mistakes and installing proven best practices."
—**Cody Foster,** co-founder of Advisors Excel

"There is an entrepreneur in all of us dying to be liberated. Yet in too many cases, society, negative news, naysayers, and self-doubt keep us immobilized and stuck. Well, that's all about to change—forever. Finally: a book that lets you know the emotions to expect along that wonderful and magical ride to success as an entrepreneur."
—**Dean Graziosi,** *New York Times* best-selling author and real estate investor

"Of course this book is excellent. And of course it's helpful. And full of insight. So here's the bottom line: You'll get more, do more, and have more as a result of reading this book than you would if you didn't read it. Success is about the choices you make, and you're holding an excellent choice in your hands right now. Take this book, read it, and reap the reward."
—**Frank Kern,** author of *Mass Control* and ninth worst surfer in California

"Right before one starts their entrepreneurial journey, there are fears aplenty. Hardy's new book helps you punch through that fear, strengthen your resolve, and prepare for what's next."
—**Chris Brogan,** author of *The Freaks Shall Inherit the Earth*

"Entrepreneurs are leading the sharing revolution, the biggest *economic* shift of the last five years. Darren Hardy's book more than fills the gap on the best methods and ways to become a successful entrepreneur."
—**Paul Zane Pilzer,** economist, entrepreneur, professor, and author of *Unlimited Wealth, The Wellness Revolution,* and *The Next Millionaires*

"The ultimate resource for fledgling and seasoned entrepreneurs alike, this book is clearly in a league of its own. Put simply, if you want to make your business a success, this is the book that is guaranteed to get you there."
—**Ivan Misner,** PhD, *New York Times* best-selling author and founder of BNI

"Darren Hardy speaks a great deal of truth about 'the entrepreneur roller coaster' and what it really takes to ride it to great heights without taking ill. There is a lot of good news in this book for those willing to do what is necessary to be part of it."
—**Dan Kennedy,** NoBSBooks.com

"Darren is the most deliberate, studied, systematic, focused, and scientific entrepreneur I know. Who is better qualified to show you the path to surviving the entrepreneur roller coaster than Darren, the publisher of *SUCCESS* magazine? Nobody! This is a book that every aspiring and seasoned entrepreneur should read and recommend if you want to succeed."
—**Mike Koenigs,** CEO and founder of Traffic Geyser and Instant Customer

"There are only three ways to make it: play the lottery, wait for someone else to make your dream a reality, or have the courage to get on the roller coaster of entrepreneurship. Darren Hardy shows us that only one of those choices will be the greatest ride of your life."
—**Simon Sinek,** author of *Start with Why* and *Leaders Eat Last*

"My longstanding economic research projects an entrepreneurial decade ahead, a challenging economy wherein entrepreneurs seize the opportunities that rise out of the ashes, as they did in the 1970s and 1930s. Darren Hardy's book couldn't be more timely or more thorough in offering deep and practical advice from hard-won experience. Now is the time to become your own business. Now is the time to read this valuable book."
—**Harry Dent,** author of *The Demographic Cliff* and *How to Prosper in the Coming Entrepreneurial Decade* and editor of *Economy & Markets*

"Darren Hardy is a lifelong student of entrepreneurship and a master of the craft. *The Entrepreneur Roller Coaster* is a highly readable, actionable, and inspiring road map on how to make your wildest dreams a reality."
—**Carmine Gallo,** best-selling author of *The Presentation Secrets of Steve Jobs* and *Talk Like TED*

"Entrepreneurs are the new heroes of our time, and you wouldn't be holding this book if you didn't want to step up and become one of those heroes. In *The Entrepreneur Roller Coaster*, Darren Hardy gives you the hard-won tools and strategies to manage the highest highs and to overcome the inevitable lows on your entrepreneurial journey."
—**Jeff Walker,** *New York Times* best-selling author of *Launch*

"Darren Hardy has turned a sometimes terrifying ride into a successful one for anyone who wants be a great entrepreneur. Learn from someone who has been there and finished a winner."
—**Jeffrey Hayzlett,** prime-time TV host and chairman, C-Suite Network

"I've shortcut my path to business success leveraging what I now call Model the Masters. When it comes to entrepreneurs, and what it takes to be a success, the master is Darren Hardy. This book is now THAT shortcut!"
—**Jack Daly,** author of *Hyper Sales Growth*, INC #10 and Entrepreneur of the Year award winner

"Have the courage to live your dreams! Let my friend Darren Hardy mentor you through the wild and exciting ride of entrepreneurship. NOW is the time to buy this book and step into your greatness."
—**Les Brown,** Mamie Brown's baby boy and best-selling author of *Live Your Dreams*

"Darren helps entrepreneurs—and those who want to be—graduate from the merry-go-round to the most thrilling roller coaster! Follow Darren's advice and I guarantee you'll enjoy the ride."
—**Harvey Mackay,** author of the #1 *New York Times* best seller *Swim with the Sharks without Being Eaten Alive*

"Pick an achiever, and Darren Hardy has probably interviewed them and parsed their approach to business. This book is like having private access to some of the greatest entrepreneurial minds of our time."
—**John C. Maxwell,** speaker and best-selling author of *The 21 Irrefutable Laws of Leadership*

"Finally, take back control of your destiny and #JoinTheRide by becoming a hugely successful entrepreneur—Darren Hardy shows you exactly how in his brilliant new book. Don't just read *The Entrepreneur Roller Coaster*; study it, and apply Darren's methods. He absolutely walks his talk and has been my trusted go-to business mentor for several years!"
—**Mari Smith,** author of *The New Relationship Marketing* and co-author of *Facebook Marketing: An Hour a Day*

"The title warns you right up front: Going into business for yourself is not a gentle teacup ride. But if you're ready for thrills and chills, Darren Hardy has years of experience as an entrepreneur to share with you. His sincerity and passion shine through his latest, *The Entrepreneur Roller Coaster*."
—**Daniel H. Pink,** author of *To Sell Is Human* and *Drive*

This book is dedicated to my first customer and the first person to believe in me as an entrepreneur— my beautiful and loving grandmother (GramZ), Francine Zimmerman.

HOW TO READ THIS BOOK

1. Don't read it.
Consume it. Study it. Devour it.
Treat it like a workbook—underline, highlight, circle, star, write,
and put exclamation marks in the margins. Dog-ear or put tabs on
the pages and bits that have particular impact on you.

2. Implement the key ideas from each chapter with the summary
Action Plan and worksheets. You can find all the worksheets
and other helpful (free!) resources at:
RollerCoasterBook.com/Resources

3. Share quotes and content from the book that strike you on your
social networks. We've highlighted some of our favorites. Join
us in our goal to inspire and encourage existing and would-be
entrepreneurs all over the globe. Please include my social "handle"
@DarrenHardy and the book's hashtag, #JoinTheRide.

Enjoy the exhilarating, fun, and wild ride!

—Darren

All human beings are entrepreneurs. When we were in the caves, we were all self-employed... finding our food, feeding ourselves. That's where human history began. As civilization came, we suppressed it. We became 'labor' because they stamped us, 'You are labor.' We forgot that we are entrepreneurs.

—Muhammad Yunus, Nobel Peace Prize winner and microfinance pioneer

CONTENTS

15

ENTREPRENEUR

Once you make a decision, the universe conspires to make it happen.

—Ralph Waldo Emerson

INTRODUCTION

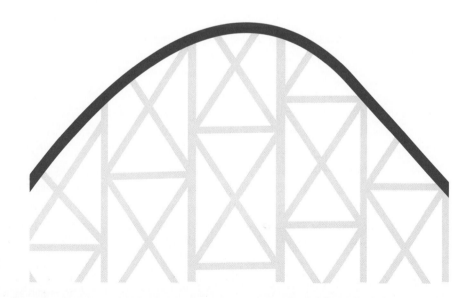

THE TICKET BOOTH: TO RIDE OR NOT TO RIDE

I n the summer of 1989, at the ripe old age of eighteen, I became an entrepreneur.

Let me be clear: This wasn't on purpose. That summer started for me the way summers start for many eighteen-year-olds. I had just finished high school and was gearing up to do exactly what was expected of me, which was to go to college.

My plan—or my father's plan, to be more accurate—was for me to spend eight years walking the historic hallways of UCLA (University of California, Los Angeles), after which I'd walk out, waving a law degree or a "meal ticket for life," as my dad put it. It was a pretty straightforward plan: I'd get a degree, get a great job with great pay, and get ahead in life. (Actually, doctor was my dad's first choice, but after watching me faint repeatedly at the sight of blood—mine or anyone else's—he settled for number two on his list.)

In truth, I'd always been attracted to doing things outside the traditional structure. I had other ideas for getting ahead in life, and working for someone else was not one of them. But my dad had been preparing me for this plan all my life, and eventually, despite my inner rebel, I fell in line. That summer, the last thing I expected was anything... unexpected.

One warm afternoon I got a call from a good friend with an irresistible offer: "My brother has this video he keeps waving around excitedly. He says it's amazing. He said to invite all the guys over to watch it. We're even ordering pizza and getting a keg!" Beer, pizza, and an "amazing," probably not-so-PG, movie? I was an eighteen-year-old male. This was my trifecta of a good time.

"Count me in!" I told my buddy.

THE MOMENT OF UH-OH!

I arrived at my friend's house ready for "guys' night." As planned, there was pizza and beer. But the movie? It was nothing like what I had expected.

I was entranced, though, and for twenty minutes I couldn't pull my eyes away from it. When it ended, I looked around the room to find my buddies staring blankly at the television screen—clearly they were expecting a different show, too. But while they appeared unaffected by what they had just witnessed, I thought it was totally rad! (Remember, it was the '80s.)

The video came from a company that offered you the chance to buy home water filtration systems at wholesale, then sell them at retail prices and earn yourself a profit. It offered, essentially, *a chance to be in business*.

Wait a minute, I thought. *I can do that*. Heck, this was right up my alley. Champion something worthy? Make a profit? Be in charge? Do something *different*?

The idea touched something deep inside me. Even as a kid, I had a tendency to see opportunity when others stared blankly ahead. In the summers when my friends worked McJobs, I did things differently. I took odd jobs, like mowing lawns and collecting nails at construction sites for a penny apiece. I was commissioned by a local trade school to get strangers to fill out surveys at bus and rail stations as a recruiting strategy. I worked hard, but I marched to my own beat and learned things on my own.

This idea of running your own business? Of controlling your own future and not being constrained by minimum wages and pointless rules? My inner rebel jumped out of line. It was like someone had just turned on the world's brightest light bulb. I was in!

The cost to sign up and buy your inventory was $5,000, and I didn't

ENTREPRENEUR

even blink. I immediately wrote a check for the full amount, drawing on the savings I'd earned lawn-by-lawn, nail-by-nail, and survey-by-survey. A few short days later, my dad's garage filled up with two tall pallets' worth of water filters. I had no idea what to do with them, but that didn't matter because *I was in business.*

I can still remember how psyched I was. I stood in that garage, hands on my hips, staring up at the mountain of home water filtration systems, and just kept nodding my head. *I was going to dominate filtered water.*

Then, just three hours into my new business, I received my first rejection: My dad couldn't get his car into the garage.

"Get this crap out of here," he said.

"But... where am I supposed to put them?"

"How about you get out and *sell* them, Darren?"

Left with no other choice, I hit the streets 20 minutes later. I didn't normally take that long to get dressed, but suddenly I was feeling something different. *Nervousness* had set in. But I took a deep breath and began to work my way from house to house through our neighborhood.

I pushed myself to knock on every door and ring every bell. To everyone who answered, I delivered my world-dominating pitch for better water, straight from their own tap. "Right there in your kitchen!" I'd tell them. "No more lugging heavy water jugs back and forth from the store. Can you believe this option even exists?"

It was a long first day in business. With every door that opened, I tried a new angle. I scared them with facts about the disgusting water they were currently feeding their families and pets. I inspired them with visions of a world where water was clean, fresh, and limitless. I used charm (or so I thought). I used compelling statistics. I used selling techniques that had never been used before (and probably never will be again). But I was determined, and I was focused. I persevered even when things looked bleak. And at the end of the day, I had sold... *nothing.*

I couldn't believe it! How was that even possible? I had 40 water filters in my father's garage at the beginning of the day and 40 sitting there when I got back. As the garage door shut that evening with my father's car parked outside, I knew I was in Big Trouble.

Worse still, it was the first time I thought maybe I wasn't "cut out" for being in business for myself. Maybe my dad was right. Maybe college and a good job really was the right path.

Stressed, disillusioned (and a little afraid of my father), I did what any rejected teenage businessman does when confronted with failure: I called my grandmother.

I was raised without a mom. My dad wasn't exactly the nurturing type either. He was a "stop crying, or I'll give you something to cry about" kind of guy. If you remember the Stanley Kubrick movie *Full Metal Jacket*, you'll understand that growing up in my house was like being in Gunnery Sergeant Hartman's platoon.

My grandmother, however, was a calm spot in the storm. She was the woman in my life who helped me become the man I am today. She provided the warm, gushy, I-can-do-no-wrong unconditional love that I needed. She thought I was wonderful even when I wasn't. All she had to do was smile and call me "darling!" and I knew I was loved.

It was my grandmother who taught me about money. She helped me open my first bank account. She taught me to save and encouraged me to "make it grow."

All of these things made my grandmother a great inspiration. They did not, however, make her a tough customer. Which meant that on that particularly trying first day in the water filtration business, she was just what I needed. I called her and arranged to "visit."

During my "visit," I gave her my well-polished, clean-water-for-pennies-a-gallon pitch. But before I could use my triple tie-down, Jack Benny close, my grandmother interrupted.

"That sounds great, dear," she said. "I'll take one."

I tried not to look surprised. *Did she just say she'd take one?*

Inspired, I pressed on. I explained the silliness of the basic model and that of course she should upgrade to the Cadillac model in my arsenal: the under-the-sink water unit. No unsightly containers on the counter, no mess. Just filtered water, on demand, straight from your tap.

She asked, "But who's going to install it? You know you don't want me asking your grandfather to do it. We'll never hear the end of it."

"No problem, GramZ!" I said. "I'll install it. It's no sweat."

"Okay then, dear, I'll take whichever one you suggest," she said.

With those nine little words, I had my first sale. And an upsell, at that!

While grandma went to get her checkbook, I started the installation. Less than an hour later, I was down one filter and up one customer.

Glowing with success, I took that natural next step of all successful salespeople: I asked for referrals.

It was too easy. My grandparents lived in a 50-plus retirement community. A nice place filled with nice people, each of whom was *delighted* to meet my grandmother's perfect grandson. Did they want a water filter? Why, of *course* they did! And of course they all wanted the same model my grandmother had.

In no time, going door to door with my grandmother in tow, I sold and installed eighteen water filters in my grandmother's building. I was killing it! I was an entrepreneurial sensation!

I was flying high. Based on my success, I ordered more water filters— clearly, my biggest problem would be keeping inventory on the shelf! I'd be able to go to school (to do that "lawyer" thing, and keep dad happy), and build my water filter empire on the side. I had it all figured out.

A few days after my inaugural sale, my grandparents went on vacation to Hawaii, and I left for college. While sitting on a lanai sipping Kona coffee one morning, they received a phone call from one of the neighbors in their complex. They lived on the first floor directly below my grandparents' unit.

There seemed to be a problem. A very, very wet problem.

The downstairs neighbors explained that as they were sitting in the living room watching *Wheel of Fortune*, they noticed a small drip coming from the light fixture above them. After the first spin of the Wheel but long before the contestants solved the puzzle, that drip had turned into a stream, and moments later a deluge of water pouring from the ceiling. Panicked, the neighbors had called maintenance and raced upstairs to find the entire apartment filled with several inches of water.

My grandparents' home was flooded.

The carpets, the furniture, the walls. Books, boxes, shoes, clothes, appliances, and more—all were ruined. The place was a disaster. And the source of the leak? The under-the-sink Cadillac of water filters, courtesy of yours truly.

I was horrified. That lousy water filter was to blame, and I immediately began mentally rehearsing the heated conversation I would have with the water filter higher-ups. What irresponsible manufacturing practices! Allowing faulty filters of destruction to enter the homes of innocent, unsuspecting victims! The outrage!

But before I could make the call, things got worse. It appeared as though the flooding wasn't the result of a malfunctioning filter. It took a qualified plumber less than a minute to conclude that whoever had installed the water filter had made a rookie mistake, putting a critical gasket in backward.

That rookie mistake-maker was, of course, me. My grandmother's perfect grandson.

It was entirely my fault. And not just for what happened at my grandparents' apartment but for what was no doubt about to happen in eighteen other units! I had installed every single one of the filters I sold. ("One-stop shop here folks! See how easy this is?") Before I went away to college feeling like a big shot, I'd placed eighteen ticking time bombs in a building full of my grandparents' friends.

In the end I didn't defuse the "bombs." It was my grandfather and a plumber (or as my grandfather said, "someone who knows what the hell he's doing."). Together they went to every unit and re-installed the water filters properly. Afterwards, tail between my legs, I timidly asked my grandfather what I owed him. He simply replied, "Consider it our contribution to your college tuition."

While I never finished "official" college, looking back now, it was money well spent toward my tuition in the Entrepreneur School of Hard Knocks.

In time, thanks to the insurance my grandfather was "smart enough to have," as he put it, my grandparents' home was repaired and renovated. I was able to pick myself up, dry myself off, and continue my water filter career. And, just as I had proclaimed that first day while staring at the boxes of filters in my father's garage, I totally dominated (well, kind of).

That was many, many years ago. But even now, as I tell you the story, I can remember that first night watching the "movie" like it was yesterday. I remember how I felt—the excitement of seeing a unique opportunity and the joy of discovering something that fit me, that suited my drive and affinity for doing things differently from everyone else.

I remember the initial anxiety of taking the leap and investing my hard-earned cash, and the moment of fear when I considered I might not be cut out for this business and might lose my savings.

I remember the thrill of seeing my first products arrive, and the deflation I felt when my father was nothing but annoyed.

I remember feeling the optimism that everyone would buy, the hollow pit in my stomach when everyone said no, the elation of selling that first product (even if it was to my grandma), and the exhilarating blur of the sales streak that followed.

And of course I'll never forget the shame, the embarrassment, and the struggle to overcome the failure that flooded my first few weeks in business.

The summer I became an entrepreneur by accident was a gut-wrenching, unpredictable ride of euphoric highs and terrifying lows.

It was an emotional roller coaster.

And I. Was. Hooked.

Despite all of the twists and turns, I soon found I simply couldn't live any other way. As I moved on to other successful ventures (and other not-so-successful ones), I learned what every business owner knows: *This* is what business is like. This is what business *is*. It is a frightening, exhilarating, and totally addictive thrill ride.

SUCCESS RESOURCE

Listen to private mentoring sessions where I reveal many of the best life-changing lessons I gained on my own wild and thrilling entrepreneur roller coaster ride. Free at RollerCoasterBook.com/Resources.

NOW IS THE TIME TO RIDE

Right now, as you hold this book in your hand and read these words, I believe we are living in the greatest era of opportunity in all of human history. It's never been this good, and it likely never will be again.

This is not hyperbole, and no, I'm not making this up. *SUCCESS* magazine is designed to serve the entrepreneur, and that means we spend our days studying the business and financial landscapes. We have access to the best and brightest business minds in the world. We see all the latest economic news, press releases, and trend data. And we're sitting on the greatest success archives ever collected in business history.

With that as background, here's my summary report:

THIS is it!

Right now.

Unlike any other time in human history.

But you'd better hurry.

For far too long, the odds have been stacked against new entrepreneurs. For decades, only those in the ivory towers of big corporations had access to the essentials for business success. They controlled the raw materials and resources needed to create products. They controlled money and talent. They controlled the shelf space in stores, and the ships, trains, and trucks needed to fill them. And they controlled all the media and marketing, from newspapers and magazines to radio and TV.

It was a game where they made the rules, ran the board, and reserved victory for themselves.

But that was the Industrial Age game. And now? It's *Game Over.*

We've reached a tipping point in technology, and it's shaking the ivory towers right down to their foundations. Every one of those points of control, once held in the unrelenting grasp of the corporate few, has been liberated by technology. They're now available to the enterprising many. So with control in the palm and in the lap of every ambitious individual with an idea and some sweat on their brow, the playing field has truly been leveled. The world's marketplace is at everyone's fingertips—literally.

And the payoff is astonishing.

In the past decade, global wealth has risen by 69 percent. In 2013 alone, the number of millionaires grew by two million. A report published by Deloitte recently predicted the number of new millionaires would reach unprecedented growth, doubling by 2020.

But recent trends show that the report is wrong. Their estimate was too *low*. The number of new millionaires is skyrocketing. Never before has the average person, without privilege, special education, training, previous wealth, or connections, been offered the unlimited opportunity and financial abundance that are available today. Never before has the average person been offered such a unique opportunity to join the elite ranks of millionaires.

And what will all those new millionaires have in common?

Almost all of them will be entrepreneurs. Just like you.

DECISION TIME

The first moment of the entrepreneur roller coaster is *right now*, and it's a choice. One that only you can make.

You're standing at the ticket booth. You can choose to seize the moment and pass through the turnstiles, or you can turn and walk away.

What will it be?

Before you decide, I want you to envision something. It's 20, 30, or 40 years from now, and you are bouncing your great-grandchild on your knee. She looks around your house in awe and then up at you with big wide eyes and asks, "What did you do? How did we end up like this?"

You will be able to say, "I was there, my child. I was there at the critical juncture in time, when the Industrial Age ended and the Connected Age began, and… "

How will you end that sentence?

Do you want to say, "I took full advantage of that incredible moment in history, and my choices made possible the full, prosperous lives we love so much"?

Or do you want to say, "But I missed it. I didn't do anything about it. It passed me by, and that's why we're stuck."

Don't miss out. Take the ride with me.

There will be people who recognize the opportunity, who stand up, take notice, and take action. Why not you?

People far less smart, capable, talented, or hardworking *will* stand up.

People with lower education, social standing, or family connections *will* take notice.

Hey, even people not as nice, kind, or generous as you *will* take action.

People all around you will become millionaires before your very eyes. Why not you? *You* could be one of those new millionaires. What's stopping you?

Is it your friends? Your family? Your co-workers? Maybe it's the haters, doubters, naysayers, and skeptics who won't do it themselves and don't want you to?

Or are you stopping yourself? Is it fear of financial insecurity? Your supposed lack of time or money? Or maybe it's the voice in your head that keeps telling you that *you'll never make it.*

Now is the time of great opportunity. I'm here to ensure you don't miss it. I'm here to help you rise above the doubts and seize the opportunity for yourself. While I might not know you personally, I know you are capable of being a great entrepreneur. How can I know? *Because we all are.* We started out as entrepreneurs, and in reality we always have been. This book is about helping you embolden that fiercely independent and powerfully self-reliant spirit that already resides inside you.

I want to inspire you with what's possible for you, your family, and your future once you step onto this ride. I also want to warn you about the loop de loops, twisters, and death drops you'll find on the track ahead. I'll even show you how to love them, as they're what make the ride so awesomely thrilling. And I will help you master the few critical skills you'll need to turn this roller coaster car into a rocket ship that you can ride to the moon—far beyond what you can even dream possible.

I know you wouldn't be holding this book in your hand right now if the idea didn't already speak to you. We are attracted to our talents, to our greater inner potential, to our destiny. Even if you don't consciously know it at the time, unconsciously you are being guided. This book found its way to you with purpose. It is not an accident. This is the ride you were meant to take. This is the life you were meant to live.

WHAT THIS BOOK WILL DO

I believe that we all have entrepreneurial roots, but that doesn't mean the ride isn't challenging. I know because I've experienced it, and I know because I see it every day.

I've seen too many people struggle with their businesses because no one helped them with things that really matter. I've seen too many businesses fail that shouldn't have, all because they lacked the clarity and support they needed to stay on the rails and master the ride.

That ends now.

This book is about learning to ride the entrepreneur roller coaster successfully. If I've done my job right, by the end of this book three things will happen:

You'll be a lot tougher. I'm a big believer in telling it straight. The first thing you need to know as an entrepreneur is what to expect, both from the road ahead and from yourself. No sugar coating. I'm going to build up your immunity to rejection, negativity, and doubt. You're going to face those things along the way, and I want to ensure that you can stare them down without flinching.

You'll be well equipped for the ride. Entrepreneurship might be an emotional ride, but it also happens in the real world. So you need real skills. From sales to leadership to productivity, you're going to get a crash course in how to get the job done.

You'll be more confident than ever. Everyone starts out scared. We all doubt ourselves. And we all skin our knees along the way. *Everyone does.* But not everyone gets help. You will. You are capable of far more than you can imagine, and by the time I'm done, you're going to believe it.

Take the ticket. Pass through the turnstiles, step into the car, and take the seat next to me. We are about to take the ride of your lifetime.

Welcome to The Entrepreneur Roller Coaster.

Are you ready to ride?

Okay, put a smile on your face, your hands in the air…

… and S-C-R-E-A-M!!!

SUCCESS RESOURCE
The 8 Tragic Mistakes Most Entrepreneurs Make—And How You Can Avoid Them. Free at RollerCoasterBook.com/Resources.

29

ENTREPRENEUR

Love doesn't make
the world go 'round.
Love is what makes
the ride worthwhile.
—Franklin P. Jones

CHAPTER 1
THE HEIGHT REQUIREMENT

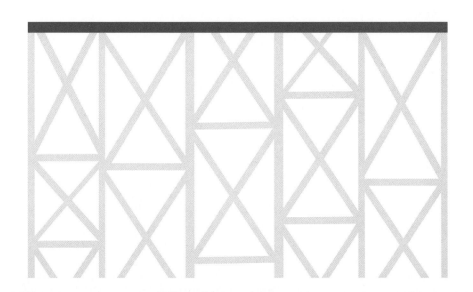

WHAT IT REALLY TAKES TO SURVIVE AND THRIVE IN BUSINESS

Walk by any roller coaster at any given amusement park, and if you look just to the left or right of where the line begins, you're likely to see this sight: an anxious child standing with his back against a lined board.

Each line on the board marks an inch, and there's always *one* line that matters the most. It's the line that marks the height required to ride.

To reach that line, a kid will do just about anything. Stand tall. Hold his breath. Stuff his shoes. Fluff up his hair. Anything that might make him a fraction of an inch taller.

Stretched, puffed, and fluffed, he waits for the verdict—does he meet the height requirement? Can he physically survive the drops, the corkscrews, and the g-forces that elicit the ear-piercing screams beyond? Is it safe for him to ride?

Believe it or not, this is exactly where the entrepreneur's journey begins for you, too—in the very same moments just before taking the plunge, when you anxiously assess whether or not you'll be able to survive the ride. And although there won't be any authorities to kick you off if you come up short, there is still an admission requirement.

For *this* wild ride, though, the requirement isn't height.

It's *love*.

Franklin P. Jones was right: "Love is what makes the ride worthwhile." It's such an essential element that if you don't love it, you're better off not getting on the ride at all.

Rock stars know it. Business gurus know it. Every successful person interviewed in the media, on stage, or on the CD that is bound into every issue of *SUCCESS* knows it, too: The first and most important factor in building a successful business is that you have to love it.

"The first and most important factor in building a successful business is that you have to love it."

@DarrenHardy #JoinTheRide

But why does love matter so much? And how on earth do you find it? That's where this ride begins.

33

ENTREPRENEUR

FINDING WHAT MATTERS

Despite my neck-jerking start as a water filter salesman, I eventually grew my business into a $5 million a year enterprise. I'd stopped selling door to door, moved operations out of my father's garage, and was leasing 8,000 square feet of office space in a Class A business park in Pleasanton, California. I had a presentation center built within the office, complete with a stage, lights, and built-in sound system—the works.

At nineteen years old, I'd gone from making my first sale to my grandmother to earning about $20,000 per month.

With that increased income, though, came increasing responsibility. The obligations on 8,000 square feet of office space were substantial, and I needed to keep growing. There was no way I could do all the selling on my own, of course—the best way to keep increasing revenue was to keep recruiting others to sell on my behalf.

One particular month I was cutting it close. The end of the month was fast approaching, and I was still a few new recruits behind where I needed to be. But even when I was just hours away from the deadline, I wasn't worried. Ever since a flooded apartment turned my first water filter sale into a disaster, my skyrocketing business success had bolstered my courage and self-esteem. I was never worried—clearly, I was born to do this.

That evening I wrapped up my final group presentation, and as usual it was Close, Close, Close. Nearly every person walked out of the room ready to make the world a better place one delicious glass of water at a time. All I needed was one more recruit, and I would reach my target and be awarded all my bonuses—and lucky for me, there was one prospect left: a woman in her mid-50s.

I brought her back to my office and laid out the entire plan for her. I gave her my grand pitch—painting the picture of her glorious new future for the minimal, almost non-existent, $5,000 commitment to get started.

She fidgeted as I sailed through the final words of my flawless presentation.

"This sounds really good," she said nervously. "My husband died recently, and I really do need another source of income. But... " She bit her lip and looked down at her lap saying, almost to herself, "This would take the last of my money. All my savings."

She paused, then looked up at me earnestly.

"You seem like a really nice fellow. I trust you," she said. "Tell me honestly, do you really think this is... for me?"

Her final question hung in the air as she held my gaze. The look in her eyes startled me. Her vulnerability. Her sincerity. Her trust. And it hit me: She had just handed me the decision for her future. It was mine to make. If I said yes, she'd give me the last of her savings, join my organization, and I'd meet my quota for the month. If I said no, she'd leave with her $5,000, and I'd be one sale short when the clock ran out.

I dropped my head and said nothing for nearly half a minute. In a one-on-one sales conversation—any conversation, really—thirty seconds is a lifetime. I knew she was waiting, and I could feel her eyes on me. I knew I had to speak.

Finally I lifted my head.

"No," I said quietly. "This isn't for you."

I paused a moment longer.

"It isn't for me either," I said.

I pushed myself back from my desk, thanked her for her time, and asked that she show herself out. Then I grabbed my keys, and without saying another word, I headed to my car.

I drove in silence for a few miles, thinking about the look in the woman's eyes and the question she had asked me. Because she trusted me, my answer held the power to change her life. She had asked me for the truth, and the truth was that she wasn't right for the business. I knew she didn't want to spend her days selling water filters. And that meant she wasn't ready or willing to do the really hard work it took to make that business a success.

If she said yes, it wouldn't be because she loved the business. It would be because she bought my pie-in-the-sky story, like many before her. And like many before her she would most likely get stuck with a garage full of inventory and an empty bank account.

I imagined her face when she realized that this wasn't going to work for her. And then I imagined her heartbreak when she realized I had lied just to make my sales quota.

That's what finally did it. It was a character-awakening moment. It no longer felt right and I couldn't do it a minute longer.

I picked up my cell phone from the passenger seat and called Kate, a woman I had just brought into the business and put in charge of running the office.

"Kate," I said, "I'm not coming back. Ever. The office and the business are yours. I'm done." Before she could say anything, I hung up.

True to my word, I never did go back. I walked away from it all—the fancy office, the (so-called) prestige, and the money—all of it. I had learned I was skilled, but I had also learned I didn't like applying those skills to anything that wasn't aligned with who I wanted to be. I had fallen out of love with that business.

And if there wasn't love, there wasn't anything.

Love It... or Else!

The best explanation I've ever heard for why you have to absolutely love what you do was from Steve Jobs, a man I would argue was the greatest entrepreneur in history.

35

ENTREPRENEUR

During an interview at a D5 Conference, Jobs said:

"People say you have to have a lot of passion for what you are doing, and it's true, and the reason is because it's so hard that if you don't, any rational person would give up. It's really hard, and you have to do it over a sustained period of time, so if you don't love it, if you aren't having fun doing it, and you don't really love it, you're going to give up... oftentimes it's the ones that are successful [who] loved what they did, so they could persevere when it got really tough, and the ones that didn't love it quit... Who would want to put up with this stuff if you don't love it? If you don't love it, you're going to fail."

Do you love it? Does your business make your heart go pitter-patter? Because if you're not crazy-in-love, you're not going to make it. You'll give up—and no one would blame you!

Even the universe-denting "Iron Man" entrepreneur Elon Musk said that starting a company is like "staring into the abyss and eating glass."

Whoa. Eating glass? What kind of person wants to wake up and enjoy a nice bowl of glass for breakfast?

Only someone who's in love. Because love can make you do crazy things. And that's exactly what you need to do to make it.

"Starting a company is like staring into the abyss and eating glass."

@ElonMusk #JoinTheRide

FINDING YOUR PASSION

"Mom, how will I know if it's real... if it's true love?"

Ah, the age-old question asked to mothers by starry-eyed teenagers since the beginning of time. It's a fair question; it's sometimes hard to know if it's love or if it's just really strong *like*. This isn't just a concern for high school kids considering a prom date. When you're standing there, back to the measuring board, wondering if your "love" is enough to meet the height requirement of this heart-stopping ride, you sure as heck better know it's real, because "liking" it just isn't enough.

What if the Beatles sang, "All you need is LIKE"?

What if Steve Jobs thought, "Yeah, I kinda like my work. It's a job."

They would have quit. Can you imagine a world with no Beatles or no Apple? No way!

You need to love it. And, just like the aggravating answer your mother probably gave you, you'll know the *real thing* when it arrives.

But how do you find the real thing?

"Pursuing your passion" is a popular phrase. It's a luxury of our modern world. When we apply it to business, though, we need to get very clear about what that means. Whenever I hear, "I can't find my passion," I want to respond with, "Did you look under the seat of your car? In between your couch cushions? Under your bed? Whaddya mean you can't find your passion? Where, when, and how did you lose it? Did it fall out of your pocket?"

37

ENTREPRENEUR

"Can't find your passion? Don't check between the couch cushions. It's already in you!"

@DarrenHardy #JoinTheRide

The truth is that "looking for my passion" is just an excuse in disguise. We use it to cover up for the fact that we're not progressing, growing, and taking action in life. The real problem isn't that it's lost or missing— passion isn't something you "find" or discover. Passion is already there.

Passion is like electricity in a light switch. It's *always* there. Even when the switch is turned off, the electricity is there, running red hot, waiting in the wires, ready to be turned on. There's no wandering around wondering where it's hiding. If you want to feel passion, then, like electricity, all you have to do is flip the switch to "ON."

How do you flip your switch? There are four light switches to turn your passion ON, and they're in your head and heart, not under your couch cushions.

SWITCH NO.1 – BEING PASSIONATE ABOUT **WHAT** YOU DO.

This is the switch everyone focuses on and believes is the only one that matters. It's not. It is a switch, make no mistake, but it's also the switch you should be most wary of.

I hear people say all the time, "But I'm just not passionate about what I do." (Add a high-pitched whine as you read that.)

I know you think you should live a life of exalted and uninterrupted passion all day, every day. I know that's what the world has been telling you. But that's just not how it works.

"Yeah, but what about Bono, Branson, or Oprah?" you ask. Trust me, if you saw their schedules—the day-in, day-out demands they are under, and the pressure they shoulder—you wouldn't think what they do 95 percent of the time is that great at all.

The mistake people make is that they judge one person's "front of stage" persona with their "back of stage" reality. Think about it: How much time per day is Bono on stage "doing what he loves," or Branson in the press launching a "new revolutionary business" or Oprah on camera fulfilling her mission "to use television to transform people's lives"? The reality? Very little (5 percent is generous). The rest of their days are spent in endless meetings, negotiations, contract reviews, lawsuits, makeup chairs, rehearsals, travel, and transportation.

Don't over-romanticize the idea of being wholly passionate about what you do. It's true that 5 percent of what those folks get to do is pretty cool (okay, really cool!). But I don't care what you do, it's going to suck most of the time, too. *Nothing is awesome all the time.* Give up that notion right now.

Did that shock you? Write it on a sticky, and put it on your computer monitor. "*This work is going to suck 95 percent of the time.*" It's the truth.

And this isn't just my opinion. Let's add to the argument the headline of an article in *The Wall Street Journal* that read: *"Do What You Love? Maybe Not. Would-be entrepreneurs are often told to follow their passion. That may be a good way to kill your passion."*

"Work is gonna suck 95% of the time. But that other 5% is freaking awesome!"

@DarrenHardy #JoinTheRide

Some people do indeed find their passions. But some passions are meant to remain hobbies—something you do for the sheer fun of it. What a concept!

Don't be fooled by the falsely exalted "WHAT" switch. That bulb can burn out at a moment's notice and leave you with bruises and broken toes from stumbling around in the dark.

SWITCH NO.2 – BEING PASSIONATE ABOUT **WHY** YOU DO IT.

I don't love *what* I do (95 percent of the time).

I don't.

I'm serious. What I have to do sucks most of the time. The never-ending airports, planes, taxis, and the endless days living out of a suitcase. The number of hours I log on my computer researching, writing, editing. The meetings, calls, planning, logistics, deadlines... argh... the deadlines! The days I spend missing my wife, my family, my routine.

I'm exhausting myself just writing about it now.

No. I do not love *what* I do.

But I sure as heck love *why* I do it.

I am passionate about my mission of empowering entrepreneurs around the world. I am passionate about helping people find success and get the results they want in all areas of their lives. I am passionate about stewarding a beacon of hope, prosperity, and abundance in an otherwise dark, fearful, and scarcity-minded society through *SUCCESS*. I am

39

ENTREPRENEUR

passionate about my fight against sensational news media portraying a perverted view that the world is bad, tragic, hopeless, and corrupt. *This* is what gets me out of bed every morning. Even though *what* I might have to do that day will almost certainly be difficult and at times painful, the passion of *why* I do it outshines any of that darkness.

I like what Mark Twain said: "The two most important days in your life are the day you are born and the day you find out why."

"The two most important days in your life are the day you are born and the day you find out why."

—Mark Twain #JoinTheRide

My life has never been the same since the day I realized my why, and neither will yours. If you are truly in love with the *results* of what you do, (the *why*), then you can navigate the tough 95 percent with grace and passion, too.

SWITCH NO.3 – BEING PASSIONATE ABOUT **HOW** YOU DO IT.

Several years ago, my wife and I hired a housekeeper, Leticia. Every morning, Leticia showed up on our doorstep with her supplies and a contagious smile. We would exchange greetings, and she would burst past me and head straight for the master bedroom. As I closed the front door behind her, I would think with a slight cringe, "If she only knew what was in store for her today." I knew about the pile of sweat-soaked workout clothes in the hamper, the expired milk in the refrigerator, the hated task of the toilets, and the minefield of dog "droppings" in the yard.

It wasn't a pretty job. But on days when I would catch glimpses of Leticia working. I'd see the care she took while cleaning the dust from the crevasses on our headboard, the meticulous way she wiped every crumb stuck to the sides of the dog bowl before filling it and setting it out for our cherished four-legged family members.

Leticia's work was the most palpable expression of passion I had ever seen.

Whenever I would discover something she had done that was far above and beyond her job description, like color-coding my ties, belts, socks, suits, and underwear (don't judge me), I would thank her profusely. Leticia would simply smile and say, "Of course." Nothing more. And though I could tell she appreciated my gratitude, it didn't appear to fuel her.

It took me a while to get it, but over time I realized she wasn't doing it for me; she was doing it for *herself*. She just loved doing things with excellence. She thrived on it.

Leticia was one of the most passionately engaged people I have ever known. Not because of *what* she did or even *why* she did it, but because of *how*. Leticia's passion was turned on by the third switch—being passionate about *how* you do things.

I love this switch because it's more challenging than the others. It's easy to be switched on by what you do and even why you do it. But to bring passion to *how* you do even the most (seemingly) mundane tasks? That's no easy feat.

People who are driven by the *how* switch inspire me to live up to a higher standard of excellence. I've seen mechanics, gardeners, toll takers, cab drivers, project managers, CPAs, lawyers, and CEOs execute the "hows" of their work with great passion and joy. They all brought the same enthusiasm and excellence to what they did, not because of what they were doing or why they were doing it, but because of *how* they were doing it. Their passion was in the quality of the activity, the execution, and the outcome.

You can flip the *how* switch ON anytime. It could be as simple as how you fill out your expense reports. It could be your preparations for a meeting. It could be the process you go through to get dressed in the morning! It just requires bringing a level of presence, joy, and energy into everything and anything you choose. Loving *how* you do what you do can be a passionate, rewarding, and enlightened way to live.

ENTREPRENEUR

"Do you need to find your passion, or do you just need to bring it into what you already do?"

@DarrenHardy #JoinTheRide

And as for Leticia? Sadly she is no longer working for us. We lost her to someone with a massive estate who tripled her salary—and made her the head estate manager. That's what happens when you flip the switch of your passion ON—opportunity finds you, and people beat a path to your door.

SWITCH NO.4 – BEING PASSIONATE ABOUT **WHO** YOU DO IT FOR

This is the means-to-the-end switch. You might not be passionate about what you do, why you do it, or even how you go about doing it, but you do it with passion because of *who* it benefits. The "who" might be your children, your family, your community, your country, or someone else entirely, but it's not you.

Todd Duncan attended one of my private CEO Forums. During one of the dinners, he told me about the tragic details of the long struggle he endured. In the darkest, deepest dip of his personal roller coaster. I asked Todd how? How on earth did he find the strength to go on, to get back on the ride? How did he possibly get his motivation back so he could ride further? He responded—it had nothing to do with *how* or *what*. For Todd, the only thing that mattered was *who*.

At age forty-five, Todd was on top of the world. He was a prominent speaker, an author of twelve books, and had built a very profitable company, making himself quite wealthy in the process. Not only was business booming, but his personal life was even more enviable. Todd had married the woman of his dreams. Every time she walked into a room, all heads turned, captivated not only by her dark hair and crystal blue eyes, but because a palpable wave of hope and possibility followed her everywhere. Together, they had two sons—their mother's pride and joy and Todd's biggest fans. This foursome was a picture of the American dream.

Excited and ready to expand his empire in new ways, Todd purchased a large company in a related field. All signs suggested that this new company, combined with the one he already owned, would be a powerhouse never before seen in his industry. Unfortunately, the signs were wrong. What had first appeared to be a great plan quickly unraveled. As a result of some transitional mismanagement, Todd was forced to surrender the newly acquired company in a distress sale. Along with the word "distress" came Todd's handing over the keys to the business, while still retaining a seven-figure debt and millions of dollars in losses.

Scrambling to recover from that crippling blow, Todd was hit again. When the economy receded, he was "encouraged" to sell his main company—the one bearing his name, the one he built from nothing with his family at his side. Seeing no other option, Todd did as he was advised and sold the company, negotiating a five-year equity deal to protect and provide for him and his family. But when the new owners found a way to fire Todd from his own company and still enforce his non-compete clause despite the agreement, Todd's once unstoppable career came to a screeching halt.

Stripped of his businesses, his income, and the reputation he had built over several decades, the future looked bleak for Todd. He spent lots of time in courtrooms with little hope or possibility of progress. Yet, as difficult as all that was, nothing could prepare him for what came next.

In the middle of the professional chaos, Todd's wife was diagnosed with terminal breast cancer. As Todd fought a long, nasty legal battle, the love of his life was home fighting an enemy of a different kind. One that moved quickly and ruthlessly. First breast, then bone, liver, and finally brain.

Given only three months to live, she battled hard. One year later, she was gone.

I remember the first time Todd told me the details of this story and

43

the precision with which he said every word. I remember swallowing hard, breathing deep, and blinking back tears. My own heart sank under the weight of his struggle and sadness—sadness I couldn't even begin to imagine. I questioned if I'd even be able to survive it. I wondered if I'd keep getting up after the relentless blows he had stood against.

But Todd did keep getting up. Five months later, the guys who fired Todd settled. Todd got his company, assets, patents, and trademarks back. "I've been battling, and I mean really battling, my way back ever since," he told me. Despite everything he's been through, Todd is back at it, rebuilding his training company from the ground up with the same energy and commitment as he did the first time around.

When he finished his story, I looked at my friend with genuine awe. How did he find the motivation to persevere? Why did he step back onto the battlefield that had just punished, embarrassed, and beaten him so mercilessly?

When I finally had the guts to ask him, he paused a moment, as if he were traveling to a specific moment in his memory.

He was.

He was going back to the moment he became a single father.

After all the chaos, destruction, and tragedy, two things remained: his teenage sons. Two young men, with eyes and spirits as sparkling and bright as the woman they had all loved, were looking to him for guidance in this new life.

"I was instantly the single father of my two teenage boys who had just lost their mom," Todd said. "I had school tuition to fund, a mortgage to pay, and debt to manage. They needed a father. They were relying on me. They were looking to me for strength. The turning point was when my oldest son Jonathan, who was thirteen then, looked at me while I was breaking down and crying at my loss. He said, 'Dad, we need you. You gotta do what you teach. You gotta keep going.' I didn't ask myself what I was going to do or how I was going to do it. I just looked at them and said to myself, 'I have to do it for them.' They were all the motivation I needed. Some say I stepped in to save them, but mostly, they saved me."

Todd's words were inspiring. All it took was one look at his powerful *who* to find the passion he needed. Just one look at those two boys, and Todd is still overcome with a profound sense of hope and possibility.

That, my friends, is what this switch is all about.

As Martin Luther King Jr. put it: "If you haven't found something you are willing to die for, you aren't fit to live."

"If you haven't found something you are willing to die for, you aren't fit to live."

—Martin Luther King Jr. #JoinTheRide

45

When you think about your business or your professional life, maybe *what* you do isn't all that awe-inspiring. Maybe there is no great mission or grand *why* to it. Maybe you aren't all that impassioned to make *how* you perform daily tasks your work of art either. But maybe it's the perfect resource to help, support, and provide financial security to *whom* you love and cherish.

When you simply refocus your mind and attention on *who* is being served by *what* you do, *why* and *how* you do it, all of a sudden your passion is re-engaged, turned ON, and the entire process becomes more meaningful.

Which switch are you going to flip?

Don't fall for the "I'm just not passionate about what I do" trap. Passion isn't just about *what* you do. You can still find unstoppable and electrifying passion in *why, how,* and *who* you do it for. Which switch you choose doesn't really matter, as long as the choice matters to you—passionately.

Once you flip the switch, it'll provide you with the adrenaline you'll need to persevere through the dips, twists, and loops of the track ahead on the entrepreneur roller coaster.

FINDING YOUR FIGHT

What's that? You're not the lovey-dovey, sappy-gooey-kissy-kissy type? Fear not. Sure, the heart-beating, burning desire to push yourself to achieve can come from a place of love. But when it comes to figuring out if you've found your business soul mate, there are two sides to this love coin. Your unstoppable drive can also come from anger. In fact, someone who's stark raving mad can be more unstoppable than one who is just punch-drunk in love.

By our very nature, we are motivated to either seek pleasure or avoid pain. Pleasure is certainly an effective motivator, but of the two, pain is better—we'll do almost anything to avoid it. After all, the number one obsession of our brain is to survive, and that means the survival of not just our physical body, but of our ego, hopes, and ambitions.

If those values are threatened, our entire physiology is wired to respond. Our primal systems kick in full-tilt boogie, and our biochemistry, nervous system, and brain functions light up like a Christmas tree. If the situation is desperate enough, we can even summon superhuman strength to defend ourselves, attack, or retaliate against a threat to something or someone we love.

But here's the trick: While our ancient brain system has evolved to help us survive, it also hides a great secret to achievement—motivation. You can hack your ancient brain and use it to give you "superhuman" powers (minus the flying and X-ray vision)—all you need to do is *find your fight*.

Almost every great achievement began with someone finally getting ticked off, saying, "Enough!" and standing up to fight. Think of Mahatma Gandhi, Nelson Mandela, Martin Luther King Jr., Malcolm X, and John F. Kennedy. Even the quest to walk on the moon was motivated by the fight against the Russians! Everyone needs a worthy adversary. Think about it, David had Goliath. Luke had Darth. Apple had IBM, then Microsoft. Rocky had Apollo Creed and Mr. T and that Russian guy and... well, you get the point.

"Almost every great achievement began with someone finally getting ticked off, saying, 'Enough!' and standing up to fight."

@DarrenHardy #JoinTheRide

A good enemy gives you a reason to get fired up. A nemesis pushes you to reach deep and use your skills, talents, and abilities to their fullest. Having to fight challenges your character and resolve. A fight will lead you to push harder, go farther, and hang on longer than you ever would otherwise.

Hmmm… sounds a lot like love, doesn't it?

The reality is love and hate are the same thing—just looking in different directions. If you love something, you equally hate what threatens it. If you love health and well-being, then you probably hate cancer and heart disease. If you love whales, then you probably hate global chemical pollution and human-activated climate change. If you love people and equal rights, then you probably hate gender discrimination, minority injustice, and poverty.

Being successful in business requires an emotional charge. Love is great, but if that charge comes from your desire to right a wrong, fight the good fight, or seek justice, then it's just as good as love and often even better.

I'll admit it: I love to fight. Fighting is an exhilarating, passion-inducing, crusade-championing force. I love inspiring people's greater inner potential and their vision for what's possible for their lives. Which is why I hate negative and perversely sensational news media and their destruction of our positive spirit and creative potential. If you read *The Compound Effect*, you can feel my anger against the overzealous commercial media that takes us for fools and bamboozles us into believing in the quick fix, immediate gratification and overnight success you'll get with the swipe of your credit card and three easy payments.

I hate the apathy, mediocrity, entitlement, and victimhood mentalities that have permeated our society. These are the enemies of my great love, and I am willing to wage war with passion and fervor until the day my loved ones lay me to rest, my sword still in hand.

One of the best days of your life can be the day when you find your fight—when you say to yourself, "I've had it! Enough is enough!" And you stand up and push back.

"One of the best days of your life can be when you finally say, 'I've had it!' then stand up and fight."

@DarrenHardy #JoinTheRide

So I challenge you with this thought—what are you willing to fight for? What do you see as an enemy to your industry, your family, your community, or your world? Is it injustice? Cancer? Poverty, homelessness, child abduction, world hunger, or needlessly expensive car insurance?

The hate of something negative can be a powerful force for good, but if thinking about *fighting* or *hate* feels uncomfortable, then start here: Think about what you love. What positive outcome do you want to see realized as a result of your product, service, or business?

Got that image in your mind?

Now, what's the opposite of that? What threatens that? What is the enemy of that? Who or what could stop you from achieving that outcome?

There's your enemy! There's your epic battle.

I promise you that when you come up with your answer you'll notice your nervous system kick in and your blood begin to pump. That, my friend, is how you hack your brain and turn on 100 percent pure, unadulterated, high-octane, heart-pounding motivational mojo!

Just like Rocky put a picture of Apollo on his training room mirror, find your enemy and let that image stir your blood. Get your heart pounding every morning so you will dig a little deeper, go a little longer, and fight a lot harder.

What's your fight?

FINDING YOUR STRENGTH

All this talk of turning on your passion or fighting the fight of a lifetime means *nothing* if you don't have the strength to take it on.

On the entrepreneur roller coaster, though, strength isn't about how much you can bench press. It's about how well you can identify your unique advantages, and flex those "muscles" to move your business.

During the boom of the late 1990s, billionaire Warren Buffett refused to invest in Internet stocks. Buffett was in his late 60s at the time, and investors everywhere were calling him an out-of-touch old fogey. Then the Internet bubble popped, and everyone was calling him a genius.

When he was asked why he didn't invest in Internet stocks, he held up his thumb and index finger to make a circle. He said something like, "You see this? This is my circle of competency. I only get involved with opportunities that are inside that circle. If it's not in there, I don't invest in it. It's not that I didn't think there weren't good companies with good opportunities operating on the Internet. They just weren't in my circle."

Like Buffett, we all have unique skills, talents, and advantages. *All* of us. There is something you do that most people cannot do as well. Those strengths are your special gifts, and identifying them is another way you can determine if a business is right for you.

One of my strengths is communication. If I believe in something—if I authentically feel strongly about it—I can transmit that conviction, passion, and feeling to others and move people into action. Over the last couple of decades, I have had half a dozen different wildly successful, multimillion-dollar-making businesses in radically different industries, from door-to-door sales, real estate, television, and online media to educational software, private equity investing, and publishing—to name a few. While each of my endeavors was completely different from the other, they all shared one common thread: My unique strength of communication was a key asset in their success.

It's a great strength to have, and I feel fortunate to have it. But it comes with significant limitations. First of all, the feeling cannot be faked. I'll convey whatever I truly feel—good or bad! I can't play poker for this reason or lie to my wife. It's physiologically impossible for me. The truth is written all over my face no matter how hard I try to bluff.

Secondly, if an endeavor doesn't need that strength, the business is in trouble.

Like a fool drunk on love alone, I've gotten involved in all sorts of opportunities that were outside my core strength. I invested in an oil well in Louisiana through a guy in Houston. (While I was living in California. Dumb, I know!) I invested in an up-and-coming jazz band and a crossover country western singer pitched as the would-be male Shania Twain back in the '90s. I put money into a biomedical clinic, a medical device company… and the list goes on. I'm getting a pain in my backside just naming them! They were all businesses I had no business being in business with.

When you understand your unique strength, gift, and contribution, you can more easily let go of everything else (without guilt) and go about the business of flexing that muscle and doing all you need to continue to build, grow, and develop it further. You can also shore up your weaknesses, and fill the rest of the seats on your ride with people who have the strengths you don't.

Remember Warren's advice. Don't get involved with functions that are not in your circle of competency or strength. It doesn't do you any good, and it certainly won't make your ride any easier.

WERE YOU BORN STRONG?

"Success just isn't in your DNA."

I'll never forget the day she said those words to me.

I was in eleventh-grade English class, and it was a Friday. I was eager for the bell to ring so I could get to baseball practice. We had a big game that night. As the bell tolled, the teacher asked me to come to her office after class.

I knew this couldn't be good.

I sat across from her as she handed me our most recent essay test, clearly marked with a big red letter that came much later in the alphabet than I had hoped. She told me not to be discouraged—that everyone has different skills and that this just wasn't my "thing."

"But even if you aren't successful at writing," she continued, "you can be successful at other things, like baseball. Didn't you hit a home run last weekend?"

I knew she was trying to be helpful, but there was something about what she said that I didn't like. Her tone implied that it had already been decided—not just that I wasn't successful at writing at the moment, but that I couldn't be. Ever. And when I questioned her, she answered, "That kind of success just isn't in your DNA, Darren."

It's true. My DNA certainly wasn't extraordinary. My mother was absent, living a couple thousand miles away, and working (I think) as a waitress and sometimes bartender. My dad was a college football coach with all the nurturing instincts of a frat boy. If you were to count up the success strands in my double helix, it wouldn't add up to much. My teacher had clearly done the math in advance.

No. My DNA wasn't special. But then again:

- Richard Branson has dyslexia and had poor academic performance as a student. His headmaster told him he would likely end up in prison.

- Steve Jobs was born to two college students who didn't want to raise him and gave him up for adoption.

- Mark Cuban was born to an automobile upholsterer. He started as a bartender, then got a job in software sales from which he was fired.

- Suze Orman's dad was a chicken farmer, and her mother was a secretary. Suze started as a waitress.
- Former Secretary of State and retired General Colin Powell was born in Harlem to immigrant parents from Jamaica. He was a solid C student.
- Howard Schultz, CEO of Starbucks, was born in a housing authority in the Bronx. His father was a truck driver.
- Tony Hawk was so hyperactive that he was tested for psychological problems.
- Barbara Corcoran, known as the Queen of New York City, is one of eleven children, started as a waitress, and admits to having been fired from more jobs than most people hold in a lifetime.
- Pete Cashmore, CEO of Mashable, was sickly as a child and finished high school two years late due to medical complications. He never went to college.

Not only did everyone on that list come from less-than-auspicious beginnings, but every single one has appeared on the cover of *SUCCESS* magazine.

I wonder if any of their teachers ever sat them down and told them success just wasn't in their DNA? Think how our world would be different if they had believed it and hadn't gone on to create and live such extraordinary lives.

"DNA has nothing to do with success. Turn your genes into overalls and get to work."

@DarrenHardy #JoinTheRide

I wonder if anyone has ever said that to you?

I have spent years studying the most successful men and women alive, investigating and analyzing the prerequisites to being an entrepreneur. Let me assure you that in all of those years of study, the details about the nucleotides in your DNA have *never* come up. Not once. Ever.

Here's the deal: No matter what your DNA is, no matter who calls you into their office, *you* always get to decide. *You* are the creator of your destiny while you traverse this planet. The mindset of "they were *born* to be successful, and I am not" is a trick of the imagination. It's a trap of the worst kind, and the only way to escape it is by creating a "success-destiny mindset" day by day, and hour by hour.

Don't let anyone else tell you what your strength is or is not. They may be wrong, and as a result their input could slow you down or even derail you.

STRENGTH TRAINING

If the potential for success is wired into *everyone's* DNA, what makes the difference? Why do some people hit so many home runs, while others never get off the bench or strike out at best? I got a clue to the answer during an interview for a cover story of *SUCCESS*.

In 2009, I interviewed "The Hit Man" David Foster. If you haven't heard of David, you've certainly heard his work. He's won more Grammys than any other music producer in history (sixteen, if you're wondering), and he's discovered such artists as Celine Dion, Michael Bublé, Josh Groban, and many other greats. Along the way he's created an extraordinary "hit list" of successful songs in a career spanning decades.

When I spoke with him, he was about to celebrate his 60th birthday, and he was still working seven days a week, putting in far more than the forty hours so many stop at.

I was taken aback by this. Most people work in the hope of achieving a *fraction* of what Foster already had. Why not take a break? Why keep working when you have all the money, the success, the fame, and the glory one could ever want?

So I asked him. I asked him *why*—why spend hours every day working for something you already have?

He looked at me for a moment, as if trying to find the perfect words to explain an obvious concept that was clearly lost on me. "On a Saturday morning, when it's quiet," he said, "there's no place I'd rather be on the planet—no exotic beach, no lounge chair, no golf course—than in my studio making great art. That's not working. That's living."

What drives Foster to continue to work and create isn't money. It's not fame. It's love. He absolutely *loves* his work. And it's that—not DNA— that makes him the very best at what he does. That love drives the time. That time creates the results.

"If you'd rather be anywhere than doing your great work on a Saturday morning," he says, "then you're probably doing the wrong thing or looking at it the wrong way."

Foster's dedication to his work and the level of mastery he has achieved is a perfect example of the "10,000 Hour Rule." In his book *Outliers,* Malcolm Gladwell explains that mastery is something developed through about 10,000 hours of deliberate, focused practice. Becoming world class isn't dependent upon our genes, he argues. It's dependent upon how much time we can consistently dedicate to getting *better.*

That might sound simple. But have you ever tried to dedicate 10,000 hours of deliberate practice to something? For most people, that's at least a decade's worth of glass-eating, staring-into-the-abyss, bone-crushing hard work! How do they do it?

It's so tempting to think these über-achievers like Foster are just gifted—lucky, natural geniuses. Don't believe it. I've had the chance to spend time with and learn from more superachievers than almost anyone on the planet, and I'm happy to report they all seem to have the same basic DNA you and I have. What consistently differentiates them is that their love and passion for what they do is so intense (some would call it an obsession) that, just as in David Foster's case, the intensity of their pursuit leads to spectacular results.

In reading a *Wall Street Journal* article about Mark Parker, the CEO of Nike, I counted the word "obsessed" *eight times.* And his obsession didn't start the day he was hired. Even as a track star at Penn State, Parker was constantly tinkering with his shoes, obsessed with how they were made and the effect their design had on his performance. Fascinating!

I have found this same descriptor holds true for many of the people you've seen on the cover of *SUCCESS*—stunning achievers like Steve Jobs, Martha Stewart, Ryan Seacrest, Venus Williams, Richard Branson, Anthony Hopkins, Barbara Corcoran, Elon Musk, and many others. They are obsessed about what they do, and they have an unrelenting desire to get better and better and better.

After years of studying the success of the world's leading achievers across a spectrum of disparate fields, my conclusion time and time again has been that those who are at the top of their game are really just people who have found something to love. Because of that great love, they have developed a nearly maniacal drive to continually improve their skills, performance, and outcomes.

But even with all the repeated and reinforced scientific evidence to disprove the myth of innate genius and giftedness, this myth will live on as long as human beings do. Why? Because as a society we *love* the myth.

"The thought 'I can't' is a lie. We use it to excuse ourselves from trying."

@DarrenHardy #JoinTheRide

A belief in inborn gifts and limits is much gentler on the psyche. *The reason I'm not a great musician, leader, communicator, parent, spouse, athlete, salesperson, or whatever is because I'm not "wired" to be one.* Thinking of talent as "innate" makes our world more manageable, more comfortable. It takes away the burden of expectation. It relieves people of distressing comparisons.

After all, if Tiger Woods, Michael Phelps, Roger Federer, Richard Branson, Steve Jobs, and others are just innately great, we can feel casually jealous of their genetic luck while avoiding disappointment in ourselves.

If, on the other hand, each one of us truly believed we were capable of Tiger-like or Jobs-like achievement (which we are), the burden of expectation and disappointment could be profound.

The bad news is that now you don't get to use the genetics excuse any longer—sorry! The good news, however, is that greatness doesn't come from DNA. There's no such thing as innate talent or genius. Sure, we each have our own unique strengths, but we can all become "geniuses" and reach mastery in any area of our lives if we commit to a process of constant and never-ending improvement.

That's why, ultimately, the key to this whole process is passion. That's what will drive you through those often tedious and monotonous 10,000 hours of practice. Like David Foster, you have to love it, or you'll never persevere long enough to push yourself to levels that the non-obsessed can never reach.

So ask yourself, right now: Where would you rather be on any given Saturday?

YOUR CAR AWAITS!

I'm not going to pull any punches in this book. Entrepreneurship is hard. Running your own business is going to test you. It's going to push you. But know this: It's *possible*. Better yet, it's possible for *you*.

Do you love it? Are you obsessed?

You'll need to be.

"Everyone has talent, but ability takes hard work."

—Michael Jordan #JoinTheRide

As Michael Jordan famously said, "Everyone has talent, but ability takes hard work." Are you willing to put in your 10,000 hours? And will you believe in what you choose to pursue every minute of those hours? Are you willing to work harder, be more focused, have deeper concentration, and do it longer, more regularly, and with more discipline and vigor than anyone else?

Those are the real requirements for success on the entrepreneur roller coaster. If you've met them, then congratulations. You've met the height requirement. You can even skip to the front of the line! The gates are open, and your car awaits.

Climb aboard! The ride's about to begin!

ACTION PLAN

GO TO THE RESOURCE PAGE AND COMPLETE THE WORKSHEETS ON:

- Finding your passion

- Finding your fight

- Finding your strength

Go to: RollerCoasterBook.com/Resources

Great spirits have always encountered violent opposition from mediocre minds.

—Albert Einstein

CHAPTER 2
SECURE YOUR SHOULDER HARNESS

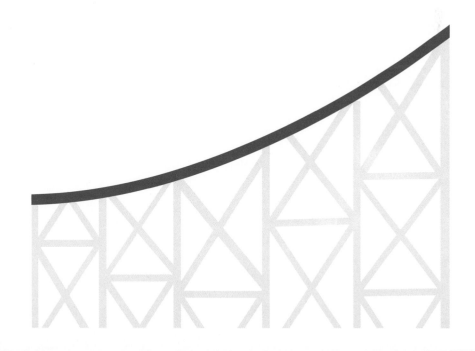

YOU WILL BE THRASHED ABOUT (SEVERELY AT TIMES)

You're a freak.

That's right. A freak. And so am I. Don't be offended—it's a compliment. Every single person you have seen on the cover of *SUCCESS* is also a freak. In fact, they're *super* freaky, and that's probably how they got on the cover.

Let's define *freak*.

freak |freek|
noun
: a person who is obsessed with or unusually enthusiastic about a specified interest

If that's not a definition for an entrepreneur, I don't know what is. No doubt you have to be "unusually enthusiastic" and pretty freaky to get on this roller coaster. Most don't have the courage to even step into the car of this thrill ride. But you do, and that is exactly why they will call you a freak.

Not only are you rare in your courage, but it turns out you're unusual for even wanting to ride in the first place—only about 10 percent of people are entrepreneurs. That means the other 90 percent are "normal."

Let's define *normal*.

nor•mal |nawr-muhl|
adjective
: conforming to the standard or the common type; usual

Yuck!

The "usual," "common type," or "standard" societally normal folks (that big, herd-like 90 percent of us) don't like it when a "freak" steps out of line. That kind of nonconformity threatens them. It challenges their choices and identity. Rather than step out themselves, it's safer for them to scorn your choices and attack you, in hope of dragging you back into the herd so they can feel better about themselves.

63

> # "People scorn your entrepreneurial choice in hope of dragging you back into the herd so they can feel better about themselves."
>
> @DarrenHardy #JoinTheRide

So, yes. They will call you *freak*. They will call you crazy.

And that is good.

"Here's to the crazy ones. The misfits. The rebels. The troublemakers. The round pegs in the square holes. The ones who see things differently. They're not fond of rules. And they have no respect for the status quo. You can quote them, disagree with them, glorify or vilify them. About the only thing you can't do is ignore them. Because they change things. They push

the human race forward. While some see them as the crazy ones, we see genius. Because the people who are crazy enough to think they can change the world are the ones who do."
—Apple Inc. ad, 1997, after Steve Jobs returned to Apple

So hello, crazy one! Welcome to the freak show!

The good news is you don't have to catch cannonballs, swallow swords, or breathe fire in order to join this freak show. (Unless, of course, your business actually is running a circus.)

The bad news is that being a freak can be painful at first.

BEWARE THE CRABS

I was once told about a type of crab that cannot be caught—it is agile and clever enough to get out of any crab trap. Yet these crabs are caught by the thousands every day, thanks to a particular human-like trait they possess.

The trap itself is simple: a wire cage with a hole at the top. Bait is placed in the cage, and lowered into the water. A crab comes along, enters the cage, and begins munching on the bait. A second crab sees the first crab and joins him. Then a third. For a time, it's crab Thanksgiving. Eventually, though, all the bait is gone.

At this point the crabs could easily climb up the side of the cage and leave through the hole. But they don't. They stay in the cage. And long after the bait is gone, even more crabs continue to climb inside the trap (they're attracted by the crowd… sound familiar?).

Not one crab leaves. Why? Because if one crab realizes there's nothing keeping him in the trap and tries to leave, the other crabs will do anything they can to stop him. They will repeatedly pull him from the side of the cage. If he is persistent, the others will tear off his claws to keep him from climbing. If he persists still, they will kill him.

The crabs—controlled by the power of the herd—stay together in the cage. All the fisherman needs is a tiny bit of bait. The rest is easy. Then the cage is hauled up, and it's dinnertime on the pier.

Like crabs, most of the human world follows the crowd. This herd mentality has been conditioned in us by academia, corporate culture, media, and society. We are encouraged to follow the status quo. For most people, that means becoming an employee. And that's exactly what 90 percent of the world becomes. When you decide to walk away from the 90 percent and step onto the entrepreneur roller coaster, you're like a lone crab trying to leave the trap.

When you choose to become an entrepreneur—to be different—and walk out on that 90 percent, something strange happens. Instead of encouraging and supporting you, your friends, family, and colleagues become crabby and start trying to drag you back down into the "trap."

"Human crabs" don't usually use physical force—they don't rip your arms off. But they don't need to. They have far more effective methods at hand (or in mouth, as the case may be): innuendo, doubt, ridicule, derision, mockery, sarcasm, scorn, sneering, belittlement, humiliation, jeering, taunting, teasing, and dozens more. *These* are the insidious tactics the "crabs" around you will use to "pull off your claws" and kill your dreams.

But why do they do it? Many of these people love you. Why would they want to hurt you (emotionally) and kill your hopes, dreams, and desire for something more?

"When you step outside the status quo, you become a giant mirror for those who stay, reflecting back their cowardice."

@DarrenHardy #JoinTheRide

65

ENTREPRENEUR

There are two key reasons:

1. You make them look bad. When you step outside the status quo, you become like a giant mirror that reflects the reality of their life back to them. They know they should be doing what you're doing, but they're afraid—and your choices make their cowardice all the more obvious. Instead of joining you, it's easier to make fun of you or try to convince you that what you're doing is foolish, risky, or destined to fail in the hopes that you will give up, come back to the pack, and take the mirror away.

2. They simply aren't as courageous as you. They can't get over the idea of leaving the security of the corporate bosom—their weekly employee paycheck and their meager "benefits." What you're doing just doesn't fit their model of the world, and they aren't brave enough to follow your lead. It's easier to mock you than follow you.

I can tell you why your "crabs" will do what they do, but it's still easy to be caught off guard by their crabby behavior.

When friends and family reject your business, it can hurt a lot more than the rejection you might experience at a job. A customer, a prospect, even a boss or colleague can criticize, question, or say "no" while on the job, and it doesn't hurt so much. It's not *you*; it's just work. But when friends and family reject your business venture, it feels far more personal. It *hurts*. "No" to your work at the office is one thing. "No" to your passion, your vision, the business you've fallen in love with is another. That "no" feels a lot like they're saying "no" to you.

What you'll soon realize, though, is that it's not about you at all. They are really saying "no" to themselves. They're rejecting their own inner voice that prods them to do more. To step out. To be brave. To take risks... like you.

"People don't resent you for being brave. They resent themselves for being afraid."

@DarrenHardy #JoinTheRide

They aren't resentful of you. They're resentful of themselves.

But it still hurts. And it can derail you if you're not prepared. Anyone who has a dream—one that might get him or her out of the day-job-crab-trap—had best beware of the fellow inhabitants of that trap. They're part of your roller coaster ride, and they can be very persistent in trying to drag you from the tracks.

This chapter is about dealing with "crabs" and other dips and drops on the entrepreneur roller coaster. It's about accepting and loving your "freaky" nature. It's about facing disapproval, discouragement, and downright ridicule, and coming back stronger and more resilient than ever.

I remember a great quote from Gandhi that I think every entrepreneur needs to keep close at hand:

"First they ignore you, then they laugh at you, then they fight you, then you win."

I like that. We win.

Blessed are the freaks… for they shall inherit the earth.

So how do you start to embrace your freaky nature and claim your "inheritance"? With the following five strategies.

EMBRACE YOUR FREAKY NATURE: FIVE STRATEGIES
1. STOP BEING LIKABLE

On the night of the 2012 presidential election, like many people, I was sitting and watching the results roll in.

I don't pay much attention during the campaign season. To me, the political rhetoric that consumes people for the year going into an election is nothing more than the net effect of the sensation-seeking news media having a field day with the public's attention. I'm not going to allow any of my time, attention, and creative capacity to be monopolized (and thus monetized) by yet another talking lizard selling insurance.

But I vote. And I like to make an informed choice. So I watch the final couple of debates, do a few minutes of research, and ask around enough to cast an intelligent vote.

Then, at the end, I love to see the two speeches—one from the loser and one from the winner. I'm far more of a fan of debates and speeches than of politics. That's where you can really learn something.

As I watched a few minutes of newly re-elected President Obama's speech, I was struck with a fantastic success epiphany. I realized why I'm not more successful:

I'm still worried about being liked.

There he was, Barack Obama. For a second time, he had been elected president of the United States of America, making him one of the most powerful people on the planet. Yet, even as he stood there with his wife and two daughters, waving and smiling to the crowd of thousands who had gathered and millions watching around the globe, election results confirmed something else: *49 percent of his own countrymen were unhappy he had won.* Yes. Almost half of everyone in his own country disagreed with him or disliked him or both—and some disliked him passionately!

Did you catch that? One of the most powerful people in the world was *disapproved of and disliked* by 49 percent of the very people he would be leading for four more years.

It was as clear to me as the skies over Chicago that election night: If you are going to be a change-maker, you need to *shake the status quo by the shoulders*. To improve things, you have to change things. Progress is only achieved through change. But change is the one thing that frightens would-be change-makers the most because shaking things up often leads to poor popularity.

I'll admit to being a little distracted during the rest of the president's speech as I worked through that epiphany. I realized right then, as Obama spoke to the masses, that I'm not more successful because I'm not pushing change hard enough. I'm not pushing progress hard enough. I'm not upsetting people and their status quo enough.

The higher you climb on the ladder of success, the more people will dislike you. Climb high enough, and people might even hate you.

Let that be okay. In fact, embrace it!

If you're not as high on the ladder as you want to be, is it because you're too worried about people disliking you? Is that keeping you from embracing challenging ideas, stirring up the status quo, and leading a life by your own definition?

Hear it this way: If all the people around you are happy with you, you are *not* doing great work.

When you stop being like other people, they stop liking you. That's just how it goes. There's no escaping it. And it's okay. What you need to understand about that disapproval is that *it's a sign you're doing something right.* Reframe your perception of disapproval, and it will empower you rather than drain you.

> ## "If all the people around you are happy with you, you are not doing great work. Progress is disruption and change."
>
> @DarrenHardy #JoinTheRide

69

ENTREPRENEUR

2. BECOME LAUGHABLE

From our earliest days in grade school, we quickly discover that nothing hurts like being laughed at. No one wants to be the butt of the joke. Years later, though we're no longer children, we may still carry the unspoken stigma of having been ridiculed by the pack.

But is it really that bad? Is it really so damaging to be laughed at? I can think of a few "jokes" where the people telling them did not in fact have the last laugh.

Have you heard the joke about the guy who wanted to build a privately funded rocket and launch it into outer space? Or the one about the guy who wanted to start a new airline—the toughest of industries—during the dot-com crash? Oh, wait, how about the joke about the guy who bought 160 acres of orange groves to build what he wanted to call "the happiest place on earth"? A total nutball, right?

Are you laughing?

Most people did when the SpaceX, JetBlue, and Disneyland business plans were discussed, albeit for the wrong reasons. Yet when all was said and done, guess who laughed last?

Elon Musk chuckled 1.6 billion times when he was awarded NASA's International Space Station cargo contract.

Launched in 1999, JetBlue was one of only a few airlines after 9/11 to be profitable. David Neeleman has 2 billion reasons ($) to smile.

Walt Disney and his heirs have snickered 515 million times as each person entered into what has truly become a wonderland.

Like Gandhi implied, people laugh at revolutionaries, extraordinary achievers, and icons… at first. So if you believe in your dream, vision, or plan, don't let the snickering and finger-pointing deter you.

People laughed at the young black woman raised in abject poverty in Mississippi when she wanted to become a news anchor. She became both the youngest and the first black female anchor at Nashville's WLAC-TV. They laughed again when she wanted to take on Phil Donahue, the king of talk shows. (Remember Phil? Barely.) They laughed more in the mid-1990s, when she wanted to turn from a tabloid-based show to positive, uplifting, and inspirational-based programming. Now, as the richest African American of all time and according to some assessments, the most influential woman in the world, it has become increasingly hard to laugh at Oprah Winfrey.

Let's look at another laughingstock. When he told his countrymen he was going to America, they laughed. When he announced he would win Mr. Olympia, they laughed. He laughed back seven times. When he announced (in his awkward, thick Austrian accent) he was going to be the biggest movie star in the world, they laughed really hard. During his *Terminator* reign, he was the highest-paid actor of all time. When he announced himself as a candidate for California governor, people couldn't stop laughing. They chuckled all the way to the polls and voted him in. Maybe that's why Arnold Schwarzenegger has such an infectious laugh himself.

Have your friends and family laughed at you? Consider yourself in great company. Check out this list of people who were ridiculed:

Martin Luther King Jr., Gandhi, Ben Hogan, Jesus of Nazareth, Steve Jobs, Richard Branson, Abe Lincoln, Fred Smith, The Wright Brothers, Gloria Steinem, Rosa Parks, Willie Mays, Jonas Salk, Bill Gates, Roger Bannister, Frank Gehry, Ron Howard, Quincy Jones, Sidney Poitier, Hilary Swank, Michael Dell, Barbara Walters, Larry Page, Mark Zuckerberg, Ted Turner, Martha Stewart, Ruth Bader Ginsburg, Larry King, Colin Powell, Jane Goodall, Sir Edmund Hillary, Chuck Yeager, Sergey Brin, Jeff Bezos, Muhammad Ali, Martina Navratilova, Albert Einstein...

The list goes on and on and on. It's time to embrace the laughter. If no one is ridiculing or laughing at you, you either don't have a revolutionary, change-making idea yet, or maybe you've been afraid to finally share it with the world. Well, we're about to change all that.

Remember what Gandhi said, because it will be *you* who gets the last laugh!

3. DEFINE SUCCESS

In *The Compound Effect*, I told the story of how I found my dream home. I was sitting on the dock at Sam's Anchor Café looking up at the mega houses that cantilevered over the tip of Tiburon, in Marin County, California—just across the bay from San Francisco.

It's an exciting thing, putting the last few signatures on the pages that make your *dream* home your *actual* home. Yet even as they handed over the keys, I wasn't thinking about what a monumental moment it was for me. I wasn't filled with excitement at the thought of moving in or waking up that first morning in my new place or even how awesome it would be to show my friends. As I left the title company that afternoon, there was one thought and one thought only in my mind…

I couldn't wait to show my dad.

I had spent a lifetime trying to impress my dad in a variety of different ways, and I'd always seemed to come up just short—I could have scored a few more runs in the winning game, or closed a few more deals in a record month. According to my father, there was *always* something better on the other side of what I hoped was pretty great.

But all that was behind me now. This house, this *epic* house, would finally do it. I had examined it top to bottom and every inch of it was incredible.

I called my father the minute I stepped in the door of the new place to invite him over. I didn't say a word about the house itself, except that I had closed. I wanted him to see it for himself. We agreed on an evening, exactly two weeks later, for him and his wife to come for hors d'oeuvres and cocktails and the first official tour.

I hung up the phone, pleased and excited, and looked around my home. Immediately, I realized I had a *big* problem: The place was *empty!* I had no furniture. No couches, no tables, *nothing*. I could already hear my father complaining, "What good is a castle if you have to sit on the ground like a beggar?" I had to fix this problem and fast!

The next day I was the first person in the door at the San Francisco Furniture Mart. In a single afternoon, I selected and bought all the furniture needed to fill up every room, on each of the four levels of that house (choosing only what was available for delivery within two weeks). Problem solved.

Over the course of the next several days, I perfected the unveiling. I hired a chef to prepare the hors d'oeuvres and serve the champagne when they arrived. I made reservations for dinner at a restaurant on the wharf of Tiburon—to which I would escort my father and his wife via the private staircase from my back balcony. I would even have them arrive at a particular time of evening so the light would be just right when I showed my father the view. It was a reveal that would make even an *MTV Cribs* homeowner weep.

Finally, after two weeks of anticipation, the stage was set, and my guests arrived as planned. After a brief greeting, an initial tour, and a few chef-prepared hors d'oeuvres, I asked my dad to follow me upstairs to my office—a room I had saved for last, a room that to this day I would love to sit in one more time. The office spanned the entire third floor of the house with uniquely tall ceilings and an angular design. Finally, standing in place of a south-facing wall… was an *enormous* window. Floor to ceiling, wall to wall, and all glass.

Smiling, I walked him over to witness the view of a lifetime.

The house was perched above the harbor of Tiburon and the Corinthian Yacht Club. The sailboats were dancing below us in the light of sunset, competing in their famous Friday evening races. From the window it felt as if you were standing on top of the world. Below and to the left of us was the point of Tiburon with its charming waterfront restaurants, cafes, boutique hotels, and green grass. Right in front of us across the harbor was Angel Island. In the distant background, the light of the sunset twinkled off the windows and buildings sitting on the stretch of Berkeley and Oakland. Sweeping to the right was a stunning view of Alcatraz with the Bay Bridge strung like a long harp behind it. Then, as if it rose from the water in front of us, was the majestic skyline of San Francisco. From that vantage point, the streets of San Francisco were perpendicular to us, slicing the city like a birthday cake. As the sun dropped behind the city into a golden horizon, it looked as if liquid gold were pouring down the streets in front of us.

It was absolutely breathtaking.

We stood there in silence for a moment while I let him soak it all in. I'd be fibbing if I said I wasn't caught up in the beauty of it all myself. Without shifting my gaze, I took a steadying breath. "Dad," I said proudly, "what do you think?"

I turned to him, still smiling, but he wasn't looking at the view. In fact, he wasn't even looking out the window. Instead, he was squinting, staring, then pointing at *something* on the ceiling—some 12 feet above us. He paused. "Look," he said. "There's a water stain on the ceiling up there."

In that moment, my heart broke.

I turned back to the window, my face feeling hot—from sadness or anger, I wasn't sure. My whole life had been leading up to this one moment, the moment when I thought I had finally succeeded and impressed my dad. Those hopes, as expansive and fragile as the glass in front of us, shattered. In one, gut-wrenching moment, I rode the entrepreneur roller coaster from my highest high to a devastating new low.

I don't remember what I said next or what he said back to me as we stood there, side by side, looking at a water stain instead of a view that could qualify as a wonder of the world. But I do remember that was the moment when everything changed. It was the instant I was liberated.

This new low freed me.

It was a coming-of-age moment. Instead of living my life to please my dad, I realized that nothing I could ever achieve would change my father or what he thought of me. In that moment, I let go of the kind of burden that some people carry for a lifetime, the burden of living to please someone else. The plummeting heartbreak I felt standing there with my dad broke the bondage I had struggled against my entire life. I was freed to pursue my dreams for their own sake. Untethered from my father's approval or disapproval, I finally realized my success had nothing to do with him. That's the moment I decided I would define success on my own terms.

WHAT IS YOUR DEFINITION OF SUCCESS?

Not long ago I had the opportunity to spend some time with Maria Shriver, who at the time was the First Lady of California. As far as "success credentials" go, she had them all. She was a six-time bestselling author and an award-winning journalist. She had even married a movie star.

As we sat together during our interview, I was thoroughly enjoying my time with this fascinating woman. I asked questions I'd specifically considered for her and a few more general questions I've asked many of the people I've interviewed over the years: "What is the one thing you attribute your success to?" "What is your most important success strategy?" and of course, "What is your definition of success?"

"*What is your definition of success?*" It was a question I had asked 100 times to 100 different people. But it was Maria's answer to that routine question that genuinely changed my life—or at least my perspective on it.

Remember, Maria comes from the Kennedy legacy. Her uncles are Jack, Bobby, and Ted. Her dad, Sargent Shriver, started the Peace Corps, the Job Corps, and Head Start. Her mom, Eunice, founded the Special Olympics. Since birth, Maria was conditioned and pressured to pursue something meaningful that would make an epic difference in the world. Needless to say, I was interested in how she defined success and fully expected an "Ask not what your country can do for you..." type of response. What I got was something much different.

In fact, in the moment, her answer stunned me, so much so that I found myself wanting to wrap up the interview, to immediately take some time to process her answer. I was troubled by it the entire drive from the Beverly Hills Hilton to my home in San Diego. *I'd freed myself from my father's ideas of success*, I thought. *But what were mine?*

When I arrived at my house, I barely paused to kiss my wife on the cheek before I grabbed my journal, found a quiet place outside to sit, and turned the question on myself: *What was my definition of success?*

I had nothing. The blank page just stared back at me.

Here I was, the publisher of *SUCCESS*. I had written the definition of "success" for the magazine. I mentor people every day on success principles. But at that moment, I realized I had never truly defined what "success" meant to *me*! To Darren J. Hardy.

I thought of Maria again. I remembered the thoughtful breath she drew in before answering the question that was now leaving me speechless. I closed my eyes, breathed in, and as the breath came out again, so did the words I had been searching for. I wrote for an hour straight until my fingertips were sore from their pressure on the pen. When I finally stopped and read what I'd written, the light bulbs started to go on, and I saw things so *clearly*. What I had always thought was so important, really... wasn't. What had previously frustrated me just seemed to dissipate. And my real purpose, authentic passion, core values, and desired direction in life became much, much clearer.

I looked at the page and thought, "Oh, yes. *This* is success, Darren."

Want to know what Maria's response was?

When I asked for her definition of success, this is the answer that both surprised and inspired me. She said, "I used to define my success by getting the news anchor job, by being a best-selling author, by who I knew, what I did, and what I accomplished."

She went on to explain that when she finally stopped to consider what success was on her own terms, it was something different altogether.

"Really," she told me, "success for me was being a daughter to the end to my mother. It's being responsible and caring for my father. Success for me is having time to parent my children and show up for them. Success is being the kind of wife I've set up for myself and the kind of woman that I would want as a friend."

While that might not be inspiring to you, it is to her, and that is exactly the point. She has discovered what really matters to her, for her, by her definition. And so have I.

We spend most of our lives pursuing success, but I'm not sure we stop often enough and ask ourselves: *What does success mean to me?*

Have you ever asked yourself the question?
Have you actually written down your answer?

"Have you ever WRITTEN DOWN your definition of success? Prepare to be surprised."

@DarrenHardy #JoinTheRide

77

My guess is no. And you're not alone. Sadly, I suspect most of us have never even asked the question, let alone answered it. Or if we have asked it, we've unknowingly allowed others to give the answer for us. Maybe our parents defined it as the degrees we should obtain or the titles we should aspire to on our business card. Or maybe commercial media defined success for us as having this car, that house, those shoes, and that watch. Or maybe the Joneses are defining our success, as we find ourselves comparing where we went on vacation or the relative excellence of our kids.

Forget about the Joneses. Ask *yourself*. What is success to me? What makes me truly happy? What gives me joy? When am I most satisfied? How will I know when I've reached success? What does it look like?

Answer those questions from deep within yourself, and you can spark real insight—an awakening to your true motivation, passion, and purpose in life.

Just a year after he was diagnosed with pancreatic cancer and given less than six months to live, Steve Jobs said the following in his commencement speech to the 2005 graduating class of Stanford University:

"Your time is limited, so don't waste it living someone else's life. Don't

be trapped by dogma, which is living with the results of other people's thinking. Don't let the noise of others' opinions drown out your own inner voice, heart, and intuition. They somehow already know what you truly want to become."

What do you truly want to become?

"Don't let the noise of others' opinions drown out your own inner voice, heart, and intuition."

—Steve Jobs, 2005 #JoinTheRide

4. GET A GRIP

One evening, early in my real estate career, I stopped by my favorite post-work hangout spot to meet up with a friend after a particularly rotten day. Don't get me wrong, there were many rotten days during my career in real estate, but this one was *really* bad. I had been rejected and emotionally browbeaten from morning to night. I won't go into all the details, but the final blow was a phone call from my archenemy, a competing and totally obnoxious real estate agent. He called to gleefully inform me that the prized prospect we were both after (a multimillion-dollar estate that was sure to sell in 15 seconds flat) had decided to list with him and not me. To make it worse, he went on to recount several uncomplimentary things the prospect had said about me—even down to my *poor choice of tie.*

Brutal. Not only had I lost, I had lost to my nemesis, who then got the great pleasure of informing me personally, and finally, just for the fun of it, kicking me while I was down. (And that tie comment really stung.)

I was recounting the events of this no good, very bad day when the friend I was meeting walked in and pulled up a seat. We said our hellos and he immediately asked what was going on. I didn't even have to mention my day—it was written all over my face.

Instead of giving me some sort of cheesy "better luck next time" pep talk, he told me about a *Newsweek* article he'd just read. The story changed my view of other people's opinions from that moment forward.

The article revealed that at a funeral, even for someone who lived a long full life as a good citizen, a good friend, a good *human*—even then, only an average of ten people would care enough to cry.

Ten. That's it.

I was floored. "What?!" I said. "You mean I can work hard all my life trying to do good and please others, and in the end only ten people will care enough to cry?"

He confirmed and then continued by saying it got worse!

The article also revealed that the number one factor that determines how many people will go to your burial site—you know, that sacred event when your body is being laid to rest for the final time—is...

... wait for it...

... the *weather*.

Yes. If it's raining on the day that you are to become one with the Earth, more than 50 percent of those attending will break off from the funeral procession and go straight to the party.

I found this horrifying.

No matter how I lived my life, how much I gave, loved, how well I lived, the *weather* was going to dictate the turnout during my final moments above ground. A little drizzle was going to outrank my entire life's existence?

I was mortified.

For a moment.

And then I was kind of... relieved.

With that single conversation, my entire perspective on living for other people's approval changed. If I ever felt myself getting caught up in or brought down by what other people thought of me, whether or not they approved of what I was doing (or wearing), all I had to do is ask myself if they would be one of the ten people to cry at my funeral. Instantly their rejection would lose any power over my emotions.

From that point on, before making a prospecting call, or after one where I was rejected, I'd often ask myself: "Would this person cry at my funeral?" And most of the time, the answer was: "I doubt they would walk across the street to even go."

That's all it took for me to stop caring what others thought of me.

I call this process "getting a grip." It means getting perspective on how important the opinions of other people really are. Most of the time, getting a grip means realizing those opinions *aren't* important.

Getting a grip immediately eliminates nervousness, worry, and fear. It's emotionally liberating, but its effects on your business will be even more profound. You'll make better decisions more easily and discover a newfound clarity. A firm grip has made my own roller coaster ride so much easier.

Someone explained "getting a grip" to me another way, calling it the 18-40-65 rule.

When we're eighteen, we worry endlessly about what people think of us. Does he or she think I'm cute? Do they like me? Is so-and-so mad at me? Am I being gossiped about? Then by age forty, we stop worrying about gossip and opinion. We finally stop caring what people think about us.

But it isn't until age sixty-five that we realize the truth: All this time, nobody has really been thinking about us at *all*.

Let's face it, most of the time people really don't care enough to be thinking about you—they're far too busy thinking about themselves. And if they *are* thinking of you, they're only thinking of you in the context of how you are making *them* look.

You don't have to wait until age sixty-five to realize this. We spend too much of our lives worrying about being rejected by other people. Don't fall for that trap. Get a grip. Don't let people who don't matter, matter.

5. REDUCE RECOVERY TIME

On the entrepreneur roller coaster you are going to experience failure, setbacks, disappointments, and obstacles. All these things are mandatory, and yes, they hurt. But it's also okay that they hurt—you're human, after all. Rejection, failure, and letdowns hurt humans. It's okay, and it's part of the deal. You will get knocked down, repeatedly. The difference is in how long you take to get back up.

"We all get knocked down. How quickly we get up is what separates us."

@DarrenHardy #JoinTheRide

I used to be far more sensitive to failure, but worked hard to reduce my recovery time—to stand up taller, sooner. Here is the evolution I have gone through and recommend for you: What used to bum me out for two weeks, I eventually whittled down to two days by focusing my attention not on the failure, but on the lessons learned and the opportunities created. Then I got it down to two hours and then to 20 minutes. Now when I get knocked down, I give myself about two minutes to sulk, and then I brush myself off and get back on the horse.

I have found that it is precisely in those moments of strife, struggle, and failure, when you've been knocked flat on your tush and you are staring up wondering what to do next, that the true achievers are born. Martin Luther King Jr. put it this way: "The ultimate measure of a man is not where he stands in moments of comfort and convenience, but where he stands at times of challenge." It is only when we are face to face with those challenges, only when we are knocked down, that we can choose to separate ourselves from other men and women, from those who stay on their backs and melt back into the herd of mediocrity and join instead those who, despite the fear, pain, and struggle, get back up off the mat before the ten count and eventually win.

Steve Wynn, as you know, is a multibillionaire and business magnate, deemed "Mr. Las Vegas" by many. He played a pivotal role in the 1990 resurgence and expansion of the Las Vegas Strip. He built or refurbished

The Mirage, Treasure Island, Bellagio, Wynn Encore, and others. When asked the best piece of advice he'd give a budding entrepreneur, his answer was, "Know there will be dark days. There will be more dark days than good days, but the few good days are really, really good!"

You will get knocked down. Know that it's okay. It's okay that it hurts a bit, too. And know that it's okay to give yourself some recovery time. As Confucius said, "Our greatest glory is not in never falling, but in getting up every time we do." Don't worry about getting knocked down—just try to reduce the time you stay there.

"If you're going to get better, you have to push yourself. If you push yourself, you're going to fall. If you're not falling, you're not pushing. Falling is part of getting better."

—Jerry Hardy #JoinTheRide

FALLING IS GOOD FOR YOU

Learning to accept rejection and to face getting knocked down isn't just about growing a tough skin. Getting knocked down also makes you stronger and better. It's *good* for you.

One of my earliest introductions to this lesson was on the ski slopes. My dad taught me to snow ski when I was six years old. By the time I was eight, I was skiing on my own. Once, at the end of a full ski day, I ran up to my dad with a huge smile and proudly announced, "Dad! Dad! I skied by myself all day long and didn't fall down once!"

He looked at me flatly and said, "Well, then you didn't get any better."

What? That wasn't the response I was expecting and hoping for.

Seeing the bewildered look on my face, my dad elaborated: "Look, if you're going to get better, you have to push yourself. If you push yourself, you're going to fall. If you're not falling, you're not pushing. Falling is part of getting better."

I owe much of my success to my dad and this philosophy. He taught me that it was not only okay to fail, but that it was an important part of the process. It was proof you were stretching and growing past your previous limits. It was confirmation you were improving. As a result, I never saw setbacks, obstacles, rejection, or even pain as things to avoid—rather, they were improvement markers on the journey toward greatness. They were events to be appreciated, even celebrated.

THE TRACK AHEAD

The entrepreneur roller coaster starts the way many rides do—with great excitement and expectation. You're so positive. So excited. So pumped.

You check your shoulder harness.
You look around at your friends and family with a big smile.
And with a jolt, the ride begins.

For the first few moments, the ride is filled with anticipation. You climb steadily higher and higher. Foot by foot you build your potential, and with each passing moment your view expands. You see farther and farther, your future laid out before you as you reach the summit of your first peak.

And then the bottom falls out.

What was once a slow, steady, predictable track turns into a deadly plummet. The first unexpected turn smashes your head against the seat back. You find yourself suddenly turned upside down and feel your stomach churn. Up ahead you see a corkscrew and a sharp turn and you wonder if you can even *survive* this ride, much less enjoy it or ever want to do it again. You wish you had never stepped onto the ride at all.

And then it gets worse.

Without warning, the ride goes dark. Now you can't even anticipate the challenges coming at you. You're smashed and buffeted. Jerked from side to side. Flipped over without warning. Every pitfall is a shock.

Then just when you think you can't take any more, the car slows, you jerk against your shoulder harness, and you emerge into the sunlight, the ride completed. Your fear is replaced with a flood of exhilaration. You did it!

The entrepreneur roller coaster is no easy ride. It is both thrilling and scary as hell. To ride it successfully is one of the greatest feelings you will ever experience in life. But along the way, you'll have to battle fear, uncertainty, discouragement, and disapproval—and a lot more. You'll be tempted to quit.

Don't.

Because there's only one thing certain on the ride: You can't get to the end if you quit.

"There's only one certainty in business: You can't succeed if you quit."

@DarrenHardy #JoinTheRide

When people dislike you, know that it means you're on the right track. When you get knocked down, know that it's going to pass, that it's going make you stronger. When they laugh, laugh along with them—after all, they're not likely to cry along with you. Embrace your inner freak, ignore the crabs, find your own success, and brave the dark days, knowing that the few good days "are really, really good."

Do this, and you'll be really glad you decided to step onto the track and take the ride.

Is your shoulder harness locked tight? Are you ready to be thrashed about? I hope so. Because we're headed for the first summit!

ACTION PLAN

GO TO THE RESOURCE PAGE AND COMPLETE THE WORKSHEETS ON:

- Crab crushing

- Defining success—the exact process I went through to come up with my definition of success. It will help you too!

Go to: RollerCoasterBook.com/Resources

Put that coffee down! Coffee is for closers only. Oh, have I got your attention now? Good.

—*Glengarry Glen Ross,* 1992
New Line Cinema

CHAPTER 3
FUEL FOR THE MOTOR

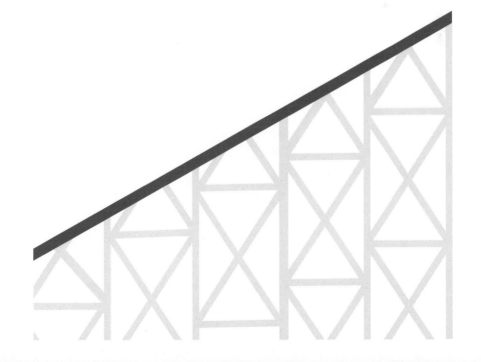

SHUT YOUR MOUTH (AND OTHER SALES ESSENTIALS)

E very day there are a million things you could spend your time doing to keep the ride in motion and your business moving. From shipping, quality control, and vendor selection, to arranging financing, invoicing, and paying the bills, there is an endless stream—a raging torrent, really—of things to do, contemplate, and decide.

Each one feels critical. Each one screams for your attention. Each one can seem as urgent as the next. When you look at it all, it seems daunting and overwhelming—a blur of scenery as you whiz past, your shoulder harness secured, your mind unable to focus on any one thing.

One of the scariest parts of this ride is deciding where to spend your precious time and attention. This is no false threat. Wasting too much time on things that don't matter and neglecting the things that do will send your cart hurtling off the tracks and headed nose first to the ground below—a short ride on an even shorter track.

But how do you decide where to spend your time?

THE CHOICE

Imagine for a moment that one afternoon before closing up shop for the day, you find a golden lantern lying in the middle of your conference room table (just go with me here). Curiosity overcomes you, and after looking over your shoulder to make sure no one else is in the office (because they would certainly call you crazy), you pick up the lantern and wipe away a thin layer of dust to get a better look. (You know where this is going, right?)

Immediately the lantern begins to rumble and out pops a big, brawny genie.

Unfortunately, this genie has his loincloth in a bunch and is not really in the mood for the standard "three wishes" nonsense. Instead, he promises to grant you instant "best-in-your-industry" status in just ONE category.

Which would you choose? For the record, this isn't one of those "there are no wrong answers" kind of questions. There *is* a wrong answer. You run through the various options in your head.

BEST PRODUCT EVER

The highest-quality and best product wins. Right? Not necessarily. Of all the fancy five-star, Michelin-rated restaurants run by celebrity chefs and those promoted wildly on reality TV shows, what's the number one restaurant in the world?

Answer: McDonald's.

One of the most competitive businesses on the planet is the wine business. After all the art, science, label design, heritage, and courting of tastemakers and connoisseurs, what's the number one wine in the world?

Answer: Franzia.

Yes, that's the stuff that comes in a box!

I have watched thousands of entrepreneurs collectively spend millions of hours designing, creating, and *perfecting* the awesomeness of their products. Unfortunately, I have also watched many of these same entrepreneurs close their doors or file for bankruptcy while their awesome "perfect products" line the walls of their garages, collecting dust.

Like it or not (and I don't) it's not a whoever-has-the-best-product-wins world.

TOP-NOTCH MANAGEMENT

Perhaps you've often thought that if you could just gather the right team, you'd have the competitive edge. But countless "dream teams" have failed miserably.

Companies like Enron, Bear Stearns, WorldCom, Pets.com, Webvan, and eToys assembled some of the most incredibly talented corporate leadership teams in the history of business. All went bust.

The movie *Ocean's 12* had one of the greatest star-studded casts ever to grace the screen during a single movie, but it grossed less worldwide than the star-less *My Big Fat Greek Wedding*. Other movies like *Ishtar, The Green Lantern, The Lone Ranger,* and *The 13th Warrior* also come to mind.

Remember the USFL (United States Football League) and XFL (Xclusive Football League)? Probably not. They lasted three seasons and one season, respectively, even though they were led by and had recruited some of the most notable talent in football history.

The 2004 Olympic basketball team was built from the ground up with nothing but NBA stars (dubbed the "Dream Team"). Who could beat a team like that?

Lithuania, apparently. The USA came in third. Ouch.

Assembling a dream team is just that… a dream. It's not the real crux of success. The right people focused on the wrong priorities can turn the dream into a nightmare. Just ask Enron.

OUTRAGEOUS MARGINS

Well, then, what about the highest margins? Certainly your accountant and CFO would support that wish. Just imagine all that profit. And isn't that the goal of a business?

But margins don't matter a bit if the product never sells.

100 percent of zero is still what?

Yep, zero.

AWE-INSPIRING SALES AND MARKETING

Apple was not the first to deliver a mobile digital media player (or MP3 player) to the market. Not even close. In fact they were the eighth, and four years late to the party. Companies like Compaq, Archos, and Creative had MP3 players with larger hard drives, which could hold significantly more than 1,000 songs before one of the most brilliant marketers the world has ever known, Steve Jobs, touted (and persistently repeated), "1,000 songs in your pocket."

So who won?

Apple.

Why?

Oh, don't argue that the iPod was a significantly better product. Certainly their brilliant marketing has helped convince us all of that. The reality is Apple won because of their awe-inspiring sales and marketing.

When the iPod was announced, the tech tastemakers weren't impressed. Rumors were that Apple would release a revolutionary PDA. Instead they "just" unveiled a music player and sales didn't take off for a long while. The year Apple launched the iPod (2001) they declined in revenue, going from 30 percent revenue growth the year previous to *-33 percent*. The following year, 2002, was also a negative revenue growth year at *-2 percent*. In 2003 they recovered partially to a positive 18 percent. It wasn't until 2004, three years after the launch of the iPod, that they got back to 33 percent growth and then dominated the digital music player market, claiming a 90 percent market share for hard drive–based players and over 70 percent of the market for all types of players.

What happened to turn the tide those three years?

Sales and marketing happened, that's what!

When it comes to the entrepreneur roller coaster, there is *one* critical thing that will keep your ride from coming to a screeching, flaming halt.

Like it or not, the one thing that matters most in determining whether your business succeeds or fails miserably is *sales*.

Here's how it works: *The ultimate success of a product or service is 10 percent product quality and 90 percent sales.*

91

Nine times out of ten it's not the best product, management, or margin that determines the leader in the industry. Whether it's clothing, cars, restaurants, CPA firms, real estate agents, lawyers, furniture manufacturers, refrigerators, or fishing tackle—the companies that become the biggest are the ones who market themselves the best and sell the most.

I don't necessarily *like* that fact, and I bet it makes you uneasy, too. I believe the quality of a product or service should be what's most important, and it should stand *entirely* on the value it delivers. But that's just not how it works in reality.

"The person who knows how to get, keep, and cultivate a customer gets paid the most. Period."

@DarrenHardy #JoinTheRide

So make the right choice. No genie needed; this is the real world where, like it or not, sales is king. The person who knows how to get, keep, and cultivate a customer gets paid the most. Period.

YOUR NUMBER ONE JOB

From the first glow of your computer screen in the morning to the last loose end you tie up before heading home, you need to be *selling*. You don't get to hide from it. In fact, there *is* no place to hide. Whether your business has one employee or one thousand, you have to *sell*.

Even if you have a sales force selling your product for you, you're still going to be selling "big ideas" to partners and "the vision" to your employees. You're going to be selling to new recruits persuading them to join you, banks to back you, vendors to trust you, and the manufacturers that make your product to speed up production and keep up the great work. You're going to be convincing people to do their best. You'll be asking people to lower their prices. You're going to push, pull, persuade, negotiate, wheel, and deal.

You're going to *sell*. All day. Every day. That's business.

From now on, selling is your number one job, your top priority, the *only* thing that will give you the speed you need to survive the twists, corkscrews, dives, drops, and inversions along this ride.

Why is it more critical than other business essentials? A few good reasons:

- **Everything starts with sales.** Nothing matters until you sell something. Nothing. You can vision cast, dream board, draft fancy business plans, meet with consultants, design a nifty logo, get pretty business cards and letterhead made, but there is no business until a sale happens. A sale tells you if you even *have* a business. A sale starts the entire process and is the first thing every new business needs.

- **Everything is sustained with sales.** It's the lifeblood of the business. Have a problem? Sales will solve most of them. And the most common problem you will run into when it comes to surviving and sustaining your business is, guess what? Yes! Sales.

- **Everything ends with sales**. It doesn't matter how environmentally friendly or socially conscious your product is. It doesn't matter how important your cause or critical your mission or how awesome your culture is. If you don't sell enough, you'll be *out of business* and fast. There are no bailouts for small businesses or entrepreneurs. There are no safety nets on this ride. Your only insurance policy is to go sell something.

If the idea of sales as your top priority every day is making your stomach queasy, then you'll need this spoonful of medicine:

Suck it up, and go sell.

A lot.

Every day.

Because this ride runs on sales.

93

THERE'S NO HIDING

I have my grandmother to thank for many of my best attributes. You already know that she helped me open my first bank account, which launched my wealth-building ambitions. She was the first believer in my entrepreneurial dreams by being my first customer (and she and my grandfather financed the cleanup costs, without complaint). Any affection I show is a result of the love my grandmother showed me. But perhaps the most visible effect of my grandmother's influence was not my strength of character, but rather my sense of style.

Yes. My grandmother turned me into a fashionister. A bona fide clotheshorse.

My grandmother had impeccable style and swore by it. "Never trust a man with scuffed shoes or a wrinkled shirt," she would tell me. It was not uncommon for us to spend an entire Saturday afternoon wandering the grand hallways of I. Magnin or Neiman Marcus, discussing color, cut, and classic fashion. "Your clothes are your wrapping," she would say. "Everyone treats a beautifully wrapped gift with more care and reverence than one wrapped in a paper bag."

It's no wonder, then, that when I began to earn a little extra money in my water filter business that I headed straight for the mall—Nordstrom, in fact—for scuff-free shoes and enough fine shirts to impress the *millions* of future clients that were certainly awaiting my arrival.

I actually spent a lot of time at Nordstrom. I would wander the racks of beautiful men's clothing, moving in the same pattern—first the shirts (by brand, then back through by color), then the slacks, suits, ties, socks, and wrapping up in the shoe department for the grand finale. I rarely purchased anything, though—I was, after all, still in the early stages of my business and most of my money was being poured back into the business and the costly office I had conveniently located adjacent to the mall. But I loved to dream of the clothes I would be wearing when I began to dominate the world of water filters.

What started as a once-a-week trip soon became twice a week. Then three times. Then the only days I *wasn't* at the mall were on the weekend—what fool faces the masses when he has the flexibility, the *luxury,* to peruse the best in men's fashion, uninterrupted, all week long?

Truly, *truly,* this was the kind of life only afforded to the most success-ful. And while my bank account didn't reflect it *yet,* it was only a matter of time, I told myself, before I *arrived.* After all, who's to say the next superstar-water-filter-salesman to join my team and make me millions in residual income wasn't waiting just on the other side of the designer underwear? So I was prospecting, right?

Late one Tuesday morning, I was well into my Nordstrom routine. I breathed deeply as I took in the familiar sounds of the piano music, the murmur of salesclerks admiring clients, and the occasional overhead paging with unknown codes to unknown people. "Paging Frederick Randall to the men's department." I loved all of it.

I had just finished admiring a pair of gray herringbone Ermenegildo Zegna slacks when I could see, out of the corner of my eye, someone approaching. He was a handsome man, about my height, in his late fifties. He came right up to me, placed his hand on the back of my arm, and asked (in a voice less friendly than I expected from a Nordstrom associate), "Can I help you, young man?"

Taken aback slightly (this salesman was more aggressive than I was accustomed to), I looked more closely at him. I wasn't sure if I wanted his help; his style seemed a bit too gruff for my taste, and I didn't trust his judgment. He wore a one-tone dark-navy ensemble that looked more like a jumpsuit than a business suit. I looked to the shiny gold name badge clipped to his pocket: WAYNE.

"No, thank you, Wayne. I'm just looking."

"I'm sorry, son, but you're going to have to come with me."

Wayne escorted me away from the racks of clothing, out onto the shiny-tiled walkway, and straight out the door to the parking garage.

It turns out the overhead page I had heard earlier wasn't really a page for Frederick Randall. It was a shoplifter security alert, aka ME! And Wayne was not a salesclerk; he was a mall cop. My frequent, leisurely trips to Nordstrom were about to become, forcibly, a lot less frequent...

"It has come to our attention that you spend *a lot* of time here. Too much time," Wayne said, his voice echoing in the nearly empty parking

95

garage. "You loiter in the men's department and never purchase. To us, this either means you are shoplifting or casing the joint for something bigger. We kindly ask that you not return."

I stared at him blankly, still in shock.

Wayne paused for a second, as if realizing that I wasn't much of a threat, and then continued in a less scripted tone. "Don't you have something better to do with your time, man? You're dressed nice enough. Shouldn't you be out lawyer-ing or sitting in an office or selling something? Not wandering around a mall."

My brain was still locked up. I couldn't say a word. Wayne shook his head and muttered something like "good-for-nothing kids these days," and "nothing better to do" as he headed back into the store where I was no longer welcome.

I stood there for a moment, watching the glass door with the worn gold handle close behind him, then slowly walked to my car.

As I started to drive away from the mall (for the last time that year), I realized that, even though I had declined his initial offer for assistance, Wayne really *had* helped me. I *did* have better things to do. More important things than mall-lurking. I had been hiding in Nordstrom to avoid *doing* them.

I had been avoiding sales. I was dreaming of sales and everything that came with them, but I wasn't doing any actual selling. If I wanted to dominate water filters, I was going to have to go *sell* some water filters!

That was the day my roller coaster ride started to pick up speed.

Trust me when I say that I *know* sales can be scary. I hid among the mannequins and mirrors in a department store for *weeks* to evade the pain and struggle of selling. Just like many budding entrepreneurs, I worked to avoid the anxiety associated with prospecting, the unique sting of rejection, and the fear of making a fool of myself. I disguised my procrastination as productivity and used all the classic tricks of the trade to escape the inevitable truth: My business was *nothing* until I sold *something*.

"You don't have a business until you sell something."

@DarrenHardy #JoinTheRide

Learn from my early mistake, and don't hide from the pain and emotional toil that accompany selling. Every day millions of businesses fail because their owners are hiding *somewhere*—hiding behind to-do lists, incessant email checking, social media monitoring, mindless meetings, or unnecessary paperwork. It's time to quit hiding and start *selling*.

Every single morning we awake, that same truth hangs over our heads as real, as fresh, and as urgent as the day before. Wayne helped me. Now it's my turn to help you: Shine whatever shoes you've got, iron your shirt, and head straight out the door—it's time to go *sell something!*

YOU ALREADY KNOW HOW TO SELL

Trust me, you know how to sell—you've been doing it your whole life. We all have. Selling is one of the first skills we learn as humans. Before we can even speak, we learn that we can influence our parents through the appropriate cry. It's no small feat to persuade a sleep-deprived parent to rise from slumber, stumble through the nursery, and retrieve a fallen pacifier or "snuggle bear" at 3 o'clock every morning. Baby's got skills! And that baby was you!

Crying is the first sales tactic we learn to get people to do what we want. (Unfortunately, some people stick solely to that strategy into adulthood.) As children grow, they get even better at sales. Have you ever taken a toddler to a grocery store? A child who wants an ice cream or a toy sitting on a store shelf will use every selling skill in the book with relentless persistence. Kids are masters of sales. They know how to overcome objections, push through stall tactics, handle rejection, not take no for an answer, and continue to ask for the order... until the deal is sealed (or until they have to be removed by force).

Think back to the letters you wrote to Santa at Christmas or to the nights when you really wanted to stay out past your curfew. It may have been several decades ago, but you were once a child with the same natural knack for persuasion.

We all sell—all day, every day. I always have to laugh a little when someone says, "Oh, I'm not a salesperson." Then they launch into a ten-minute, detailed "sales" presentation—complete with bullet points and case studies—selling me on the fact that they're no good at selling.

We all make a dozen sales presentations every day. We sell a friend to go see a particular movie or try a new restaurant. We sell why we're late for an event or can't make a party. We even sell ourselves on why we should skip a workout or buy something we don't need.

And if you're a parent? You're working overtime refining and mastering your selling skills. You're constantly selling your kids on something. "Eat your vegetables." "Use your words." "Don't hurl yourself off the back of the couch." "Texting and driving will kill you." If you're a parent, your sales skills are already in heavy use.

Don't fool yourself. Everyone sells. Even you.

So grab your headband and water bottle. We're about to do some P90X on your sales muscles.

> ## "In today's age you're not competing only with competitors. You're competing with prospects, friends, and their adorable baby pictures."
>
> @DarrenHardy #JoinTheRide

BUILDING YOUR SALES MUSCLES: NINE STEPS

Just because everyone sells doesn't mean we don't need to get better at it. In a world awash in sales solicitations, your prospects are far savvier than they used to be. Consumers have become very good at avoiding marketing and advertising. They're skipping commercials, turning a blind eye to website banners, and passing right by billboards without seeing them. Our culture has become so overwhelmed by commercial sales messages that we have become immune to most of them. And in today's age, you are not competing only with competitors. You are competing with prospects, friends, and their adorable baby pictures.

Now more than ever, the fate of your business, your dreams, and your future hinges on your ability to sell better than your competition. Otherwise your roller coaster ride is going to come to a screeching, whiplash-inducing halt. The rest of this chapter is dedicated to equipping you with the standout sales strategies that, when used, will break any previous roller coaster speed records.

So put that coffee down, and let's get started!

1. DON'T KILL YOUR CUSTOMERS

After I started my real estate business, I would occasionally meet with a man who became an unofficial mentor to me in the industry. I liked his style and admired how easy he made it all look—as if buying a multimillion-dollar home was the most obvious choice any of his prospects could make. I also admired his watch, his car, his home—well, all of his homes—and everything else that went along with being a wildly successful entrepreneur.

This man was the most skilled salesman I knew at the time, and I wanted to hear anything he had to say. One day we met for lunch, and I expressed my frustration with my latest sales numbers. They just weren't where I knew they could be, and I couldn't figure out why.

"Let me see your prospect list," he said.

I opened my briefcase, pulled out a file, and pushed it across the table to him. "These are the prospects in my sights right now," I said, ambition dripping off every word. He raised an eyebrow at my comment and, looking down, opened the folder.

Inside was my prospect list. It was a few sheets of worn paper with listing names and contact information recorded on them. In many ways, this list was my prized possession. My future success (or failure) was dependent on what happened with the names in this file. At the top, in thick black marker, I'd written "HIT LIST."

He raised another eyebrow.

"Well," he said and pushed the file back to me, "I can see the problem."

"What is it?" I looked down at the list, anxious to know. Did I not have the right information for my prospects? Were there too few? Was I not being aggressive enough?

He leaned in and squinted his eyes in the way masters do when they're about to impart great wisdom to their pupils.

"Let me ask you this: If I had a list like this and your name was on it and you *saw* it… how would you feel? How would you feel about being on my *hit list?* About being *in my sights* like you were looking at me up the barrel of a loaded gun?"

I quickly closed the folder and shrugged like a kid being chastised for skipping school.

"No one wants to be your next hit, Darren. They don't want to be your next victim. And when you label them that way, you *think* of them that way. And when you think of people that way, you treat them that way. They *know* it and feel it. They can tell."

He pulled a pen from his pocket, reached over, and reopened the file folder. He crossed out "HIT LIST," and with a fast and steady hand wrote, "Families I'm Going to Help Next."

"Now," he said, placing the pen back in his suit coat, "get back out there. You'll notice a difference right away."

He was right. I immediately began to see a difference in how I approached people and, more important, how they responded. Before I picked up the phone, I'd look at my list and I'd think about the family I was calling. What did they need help with? Were they struggling in a home they couldn't afford? Did they need a bigger house now that they had children—one in a better school district? Were they first-time buyers overwhelmed and nervous by the thought of such a large purchase?

As soon as I shifted my perspective, my success rate improved dramatically, and my sales shot up. But the best part of all? I really began to enjoy the process. What had started out as an exercise in sheer brute force had become something I felt good about—for more than just the size of my commission.

What my mentor was doing, I realize now, was reframing the whole idea of sales. He could have changed my "pitch" or my wording, but he knew that what people were really responding to was my misdirected intention. Whereas before I had always thought of sales as a way to *get* something, I could now see it as a tool for *giving*. For the first time, I began to understand the strange, wonderful irony that sales isn't about selling at all.

Sales are critical to grow your business. But if you make only one change in your sales strategy, make it this: *Stop selling*.

Really. Stop it right now.

You're killing yourself and your customers. You are alienating the people who might love what you have to offer, and you're missing out on the huge upside of using your product or service as a tool for helping others.

If you're the type of person who's always thought of "sell" as a four-letter word, this is good news for you. You can now replace that with another four-letter word: HELP. How can you help? How does your product or service address someone's deepest need or fear? What problem does it solve? How does it make a positive difference?

"Want to sell more? Stop selling. Help instead."

@DarrenHardy #JoinTheRide

Don't sell—HELP.

And if what you have *doesn't* help?

Then you've either got the wrong prospect or the wrong product.

101

2. GET IN BED WITH YOUR CUSTOMER

Once you have reframed the entire notion of sales—once you start focusing on what your prospects want versus what you want from your prospects—it's time to change the messaging to match your change of heart.

To help you do that, let me ask you this: What do you think is the number one quality of the most effective sales and marketing messages?

Passion?

Enthusiasm?

Conviction?

Urgency?

Desire?

Nope.

It's *empathy.*

Now that you've got your prospects out of your crosshairs, it's time to get in their beds—mentally, of course! If you want your sales and marketing messaging to connect with people on a gut level, if you want to grab their hearts and move them into action, then you have to get in their gut. To connect *with*, not just communicate *to* your audience, you have to feel what they feel, experience what they experience, and think like they think.

When I teach this strategy to CEOs and leadership teams of high-growth companies, I simply tell them to crawl into the bed of their client and imagine what they are thinking and feeling. At the end of a long day… in those few moments before their eyes close and they drift off to sleep, what are they thinking about? Seriously, ask yourself:

What are they thinking about?

What are they worried about?

Who are they worried about?

What do they fear?

Who do they fear?

What do they hope for?
Who do they hope to impress?
What are their desires, ambitions, and goals?
What do they think they need help with?
What resources, ideas, or assistance are they looking for to overcome their unspoken fears or accomplish their innermost desires?

Don't just think about these questions, *feel* them. Climb into their beds and into the worries of their minds and the hopes of their hearts. Write down what you feel, and be as descriptive and raw as possible.

After you answer those questions from the viewpoint of your prospective client, look back at what you wrote. Examine the specific language you used to describe those feelings and thoughts.

You will find much of your best sales and marketing language in those words—language that shows *you know who they are, who they are trying to become, and what they are trying to do.* You will create language that is rich with empathy. With it, you'll be able to speak from their perspective and straight to their hearts from your own.

3. DON'T BE A FIRST DATE FRED

Back in my early twenties when I was living the bachelor life in Southern California, I had a buddy we called "First Date Fred." Fred was a nice, good-looking guy, wrapping up his first year of med school. He was also desperate to find the perfect girl and fall madly in love. Every night of every weekend you could find Fred at one of the fancy beachside hotspots wining and dining another beautiful woman. Fred seemed to have it all figured out.

The problem was that while Fred had a date every weekend, he *never* had a second date. Ever! Fred would have one amazing evening (he always claimed it was amazing) and then never hear from her again. Ever! His first dates wouldn't return his calls. They'd avoid him at the local hangouts. And there was more than one awkward instance in line at the grocery store.

One day at the gym, in an effort to solve the second-dateless mystery, one of our other buddies saw one of the (many) women who never called and asked, point-blank, *why*.

"You know," she said, "he was a nice guy and certainly nice to look at… but he didn't ask a single question about *me*. He just kept *talking*. He told me how he wanted to find a woman and treat her like a queen and how he didn't want the woman he married to have to work another day in her life. He told me how many kids he wanted and the neighborhood he wanted to move to. He said that everyone says he's the perfect guy, and they're shocked that he's still single. But the kicker? It was when he told me he thought we really had a future together! He barely knew my *name*, much less anything that mattered to me.

"I don't need to be treated like a queen," she clarified. "And I own my own clothing boutique, so I plan to keep working. He made some pretty broad assumptions about me and got it totally wrong."

She wasn't buying what Fred was selling because Fred was selling *all wrong*.

Fred isn't the only one who screws this up. I was working with a CEO recently, and he said, "I want my marketing message to speak what is in my heart."

I responded, "No, you don't."

Have you ever been subjected to someone's passionate (probably long-winded) pitch about something they're all fired up about but that you couldn't care less about?

"Sales is filling a customer's perceived need, not your need to sell something."

@DarrenHardy #JoinTheRide

Yeah, me too. It's painful.

Undaunted, the CEO said, "I see a great need for this in the market."

I said, "Then that makes one of you."

He was making the same, common mistake that so many First Date Freds and entrepreneurs do: focusing on what *they* are passionate about and the need *they* see. They're following the old sales adage of "finding a need and filling it."

Well, Fred, the old sales adage is wrong. Sales is *not* about finding a need and filling it. Imagine that you sell cars and see someone driving around an old relic. "Seeing a need," you approach the guy to pitch him on the fact that his car is old, ugly, and beat up, and it's time for a new one. Guess what? You might get beat up yourself. It turns out he *loves* his old classic. It was his grandfather's, and he remembers driving to the lake with him in it every summer. It's one of his most prized possessions. You might as well have called his child ugly.

No. Sales—*effective* sales—is not "finding a need and filling it." Effective sales is about finding a *perceived* need and *helping* someone fulfill it. If the customer doesn't perceive the need, *there is no need*.

The misguided drive to "create" a need is why we see so much chest-beating, egocentric marketing out there. It's obnoxious, exhausting, and what's worse, it's ineffective. Don't be a First Date Fred.

Pull—don't push.

Investigate—don't present.

Probe—don't pitch.

Ask—don't assume.

How?

Talk less—listen more.

Make fewer statements—ask more questions.

If you want to master one skill that will skyrocket your sales success, learn how to ask better questions, not how to do a better presentation. Ask questions, find answers that serve as solutions, and *then* (only then) build your presentation or sales message around the answers you receive.

As soon as we figured out *that* was where First Date Fred was going wrong, we put him through his first sales training (something they didn't teach him in med school). Shortly after, Fred met a great woman, and, yes, he even secured his first second date. After asking her many questions, properly assessing her needs, and determining that he could fulfill them, he made the biggest pitch of his life.

She said yes. She's now Mrs. Fred.

4. SELL LIKE JOHN LENNON

I have a real estate agent in South Beach, Miami, whose name is John Lennon. (Really. That's his name.) In the past 19 years, John has sold more than $3.7 billion in real estate. *Three billion.* If you do the math on his 3 percent commission, he's done almost as well as the other Lennon!

What's even more impressive, though, is that he's sold all that real estate on a *single street* in just *six* buildings.

John sells on a street named South Pointe Drive, located in an exclusive area called SoFi (South of Fifth) in South Beach. His sales territory consists of six über-luxury high-rises along the cruise ship waterway and Miami Beach front. That's it. One street. Six buildings. Three billion dollars.

"Well," you might be thinking, "of *course* he's selling like a rock star. The price per square foot would make anyone as wealthy as a Beatle." Stop right there—don't be fooled by the ZIP code. The prices are high, but so is the competition. There are hundreds of agents trying to work in John's area, and he's outselling all of them many, *many* times over.

John took my wife, Georgia, and me to lunch, and I was pressing him to share some of his story. He's clearly at the top of his game, and of course I was curious to know how he did it.

"When I started out," he told us, "I was in an office with four other agents. We took turns handling incoming foot traffic, and we all had the same number of prospects to work with. Each of the other four would close a deal once every three to four months. I mean, these are big sales, and they don't necessarily happen every day—for most people. But I was closing 31 per month. One a day."

I'm pretty sure I choked on my iced tea when he said it. I mean, I had a pretty solid run in real estate myself but couldn't imagine closing

31 multimillion-dollar deals a month!

"How do you explain the difference?" I asked. "You've got the same leads, the same territory, and even the same apartment units. But you're getting completely different results."

"The difference is… " he paused as he wiped his mouth and placed his napkin on his plate. This was about to get serious, I could tell. "I don't sell what they sell."

Georgia and I exchanged glances—we knew John sold high-end condominiums and that his competition sold the exact same units. How could he be selling something *different*?

Sensing our confusion (and clearly entertained by it), John Lennon explained: "Sure, we sell the same buildings and the same units, even, but *I* sell something different for every different person."

I knew the next words out of his mouth were going to rock my world—and I was right.

"One time," he continued, "the building developer called to ask what I had sold that day. I said, 'I sold a $4 million parking space, a $2.8 million gym and spa access pass, and a $6 million closet. And each came with an apartment included. The developer said, 'What do you mean you sold a $4 million parking space?'"

John went on to explain to the developer that in each case he discovered what was most important to each client. Take the parking space, for example. The buyer had vintage cars and had a bad experience in a previous building. John spent an hour explaining the security, safety, and cleanliness of the underground parking. "The buyer couldn't write the check fast enough," John said.

The secret to John Lennon's success, and to *your* success in sales, is that he is the ultimate Connector. John finds his client's most important desire, need, or hot button and *connects* the solution he has to meet it.

We've already discussed the importance of asking questions and listening to the answers. But simply asking questions for curiosity's sake is not going to earn you an income worthy of a multi-platinum artist. If, after the questioning is done, you launch into your same old First Date Fred pitch, you'll end up like one of the other four guys in Lennon's office with nothing but a wide-open schedule and a gaping hole in your bank account.

The true genius behind "Selling like Lennon" is that once John figures out what is most important to his prospects, he focuses all of his effort and education on their number one need or desire. Then, when the time comes to show the unit or "make the sale," the same unit in the same building that's been shown many times is transformed into something entirely new, totally different, and completely personalized to the client walking through it in that moment.

By approaching each sale in this way, John is not limited by the number of buildings or units. His options for closing a deal are as vast and varied as the people looking for real estate in Miami, which (if you've spent any time in South Beach, you know) are *infinite*.

So let me ask you: Are you selling like Lennon? Do you *connect* to your customers by asking questions and genuinely listening to the answers? And if so, do you take the extra step to *connect* those customers to expertly personalized solutions? Do you take time to drastically adjust your message to meet each individual customer's needs?

If not, it's time to get started. After all, "You were only waiting for this moment to arise...." (get it?)

5. FIND A BRIDGE

If I were to guess, I'd bet someone, somewhere told you that in order to excel at sales, you have to get good at making cold calls. Yuck! Even the words "cold call" send shivers up my spine —not because of the temperature, but because making cold calls is awful. I bet you feel the same way, dreading picking up that phone only to hear the disdain in the voice on the other end.

If that's the case, then you'll love this: *Don't make cold calls.*

I don't make cold calls (anymore). You shouldn't, either. No one should make cold calls (I learned). Cold calls are for rookies, and you don't want to be a rookie.

"Cold calls are for rookies. Don't be a rookie. Find a relationship bridge."

@DarrenHardy #JoinTheRide

There is no reason to waste your time (and it's irresponsible to waste the time of the person you're calling on) when there is a very easy way to warm that chilly prospect up. You need to find a bridge.

I'm contacted a dozen times a week by someone asking me to endorse his or her book. If I don't know the person or their work personally, I can't even take the time to respond. The amount of time I would spend on the "not at this time, best of luck on your future success" emails alone would burn entire afternoons. That's time I just can't afford to lose.

But recently Harvey Mackay, a colleague whom I trust and respect, asked me to review a book by his friend. It was a simple request: Read it, and if I liked it, would I please provide an endorsement. I did, and I did. And it was the only book I endorsed that month. The rest might have been worthy, but the rest were not referred to me by an already trusted source.

Rather than just being some Joe or Jane Shmoe contacting important prospects cold and out of the blue (classifying you as a rookie in their mind), find a relationship bridge between you and your desired client. Get referred from a credible and trusted source.

Brainstorm who knows the person or company you want to do business with. If you don't know anyone right now (be sure to check your LinkedIn connections), then find out who their vendors are (CPA, attorney, etc.). Find someone to get you personally introduced.

In today's world you are no more than two to three degrees from just about anyone on the planet. Identify those two or three dots to connect, and walk confidently across that bridge. They'll likely be happy to see you when you get to the other side.

6. SELL IN BULK

I recently had lunch with a CEO friend, Mark, who owns a commercial construction management company valued at about half a billion dollars. I negotiated to pay the lunch tab if he'd tell me the secret to his fantastic success. So for the price of a spinach and strawberry salad with salmon, Mark told me the story of discovering the greatest sales strategy of his career—a strategy he stumbled upon while trying to impress a girl (of course).

It was the spring of his sophomore year of high school, and the season of the annual Student Council candy bar drive. The seller of the most candy bars would win a trip to Washington, D.C., and Mark was in it to win it. Not the trip to D.C., mind you. He didn't care much for history or politics. Mark's motivation for winning was Cindy Mason, the reigning candy bar champ.

Cindy was a senior and the most popular, most beautiful girl in school. She also had a three-year candy bar sales winning streak and a burning desire to close her career 4 and 0. With typical 15-year-old guy-logic, Mark thought winning the candy bar drive would capture Cindy's attention and affection. Misguided? Perhaps. Nevertheless, Mark was determined.

As soon as he got his first box, Mark approached his three best friends who, instead of buying candy bars, convinced Mark to give them candy bars for free. Mark then went to his brother and sister, who went "half-sies" on one bar. His calorie-counting parents turned him down flat, explaining he needed to figure it out on his own (parents, take note).

In just one afternoon, Mark had exhausted his entire network, and his sales were in the red. Meanwhile, Cindy Mason had candy bars flying out of her locker… and was still oblivious to the fact that Mark even existed.

Despite these setbacks however, Mark's determination did not falter. Instead, he suspected he needed to take a different approach. One night, his parents had their friends Bob and Nancy over for dinner. Mark suggested candy bars for dessert (for the bargain price of only $1 each). With caramel dripping down his chin, Bob said, "You know, Mark, these are really good. If you give me a box, I could probably sell them at my office."

Sold!

The next day, Bob came back with an empty box, an envelope full of cash, and a request for more.

As he pulled another box of bars from his backpack and handed them over to Bob, Mark knew he was onto something. Instead of trying to sell candy bars one by one, he would sell them box by box. He immediately began targeting several more of his parents' friends who had access to offices filled with candy lovers. Daily, these well-connected people emptied boxes of candy for him and returned with envelopes of cash begging for more chocolate-caramel goodness.

Mark not only won the candy drive, he crushed the school's sales record, including that of the previously undefeated Cindy Mason.

Unfortunately, contrary to Mark's original hope, Cindy was *not* impressed. In fact, she was so unimpressed that she made it her mission to see that no girl at Mark's high school would be caught dead with him on a date. Mark's winning strategy had cost him the girl and sentenced him to many a date-less Friday night, but he didn't care (not much, at least). Mark had gained something much greater, discovering the single most important sales strategy of his professional career.

Aside from those first few failed candy bar sales attempts, Mark has *never* sold accounts one by one. In the decades since crushing the candy bar contest, Mark has looked instead for influencers: people with their own large networks who, if sold on his idea, venture, or opportunity, could potentially generate entire *volumes* of transactions for him. Not just one. Time and again, this strategy has worked, and Mark has millions in the bank to show for it.

Take that, Cindy Mason.

If you really want to add some speed to your roller coaster ride, shift your thinking. Instead of taking each sale one by one, use the Mark

111

approach and sell in bulk, box by box. Seek out influencers, those who are connected to broader networks of potential customers. Sure, it might mean you don't have a date to the movies, but sometimes that's the price of success.

7. DELIVER SHOCK AND AWE

I started selling real estate when I was just twenty years old. I was the youngest in my office by twenty years, but I didn't let that hold me back. What I lacked in age and experience, I made up in hustle and aggressiveness. I knew that if I was going to be successful, I was going to have to go big. So I developed a plan.

The most competitive prospecting group for a Realtor is expired listings. Expired listings are homes that were listed with a different agent, but the home didn't sell and the contract expired. When this happens, an alert shows up on the Multiple Listing Service notifying all other agents that this listing is back up for grabs! Immediately several dozen real estate agents pounce and start calling on the owners who were unable to sell their home with "the other guy."

It was tough to stand out in the sea of hungry agents who, in a two-hour window, were all laying on their best pitch. It was competitive for sure, but if you can rise above the madness and clutter, expired listings can be very lucrative.

I knew this, so I developed what I called my Shock and Awe Blitz Campaign. Once I set my sights on you, you were either going to love me or hate me. But two things were certain: You would not be able to ignore or forget me.

The campaign went like this. Between 6:00 and 7:00 a.m. the morning your listing expired, I'd be standing on your doorstep asking to re-list your home with me (immediately separating myself from everyone else and delivering a little shock). Sometimes this was all it took, but if not...

Later that day you would get a package hand-delivered by an assistant—a package that we affectionately called "Da-Bomb" because it was big and stuffed full of combustible materials explaining why I was "Da-Bomb."(Cheesy, yes, but it worked!) And if it didn't...

Then in the early evening, an assistant would show up, hand them a SOLD sign, and say, "This is a gift from Darren Hardy—you'll need it soon after you hire him to sell your house." (Boom!)

Later that evening, I would stop by in person and ask for the listing again. If the listing *still* hadn't been secured, I would have something hand-delivered or mailed to them every day for at least two weeks along with a daily call or visit from me personally.

It wasn't long before they would call exasperated, exclaiming that if I would market their house like I marketed myself, I had the job.

I'll admit that my Shock and Awe campaign was a little extreme. But this isn't about aggressiveness for aggressiveness' sake. In competitive markets, things happen quickly. In real estate, for example, when it comes to expired listings, more than 50 percent of the time the listing is won or lost within the first 24 hours. That little window of time means you can't be casual unless you want to be a *casualty*.

Will you lose some prospects this way? Certainly. And that's okay.

Maybe the best sales advice I ever got was from this mega-successful mortgage broker named Mari Mahoney. She did more business than any ten "successful" mortgage agents combined. When I asked her how she did it, she quickly responded, "I lose one out of five for being too aggressive." She paused for effect, then added, "But I get the other four!"

"You lose 1 out of 5 prospects for being too aggressive. But you win the other 4!"

@DarrenHardy #JoinTheRide

That statement changed my life.

Before then I was overly concerned about being too assertive or overbearing. If someone got mad or called the broker (my dad!) to complain that I was calling too early or too late or showing up on the doorstep too often, I was horrified. After my lunch with Mari, being aggressive became my goal.

Ask yourself this: Are you shocking enough in your approach? Are you awe-inspiring? If not, it's time to stop being scared of scaring clients away. Instead, be excited about the customers who will admire your willingness to go big!

8. SELL TO THE BEST, FORGET THE REST

The challenge with shock and awe is that it uses up a lot of resources. After all, you can't be standing on everyone's porch at 6:00 in the morning. To maximize your efforts, you need to narrow your sights and go after the "best buyers."

Best buyers are about 10 percent of your client base, and you can probably picture them in your mind:

They love your product or service.
They buy your best products.
They buy in bigger quantities.
They buy frequently.
They're a joy to work with.
They love to tell their friends about you.

What's magical about those best buyers is that even though they only make up 10 percent of your client base, they generate 90 percent of your profits! And the rest? They generate 100 percent of the headaches.

As a result, just one best buyer can be worth 100 times an average one. That makes the solution easy: *Spend 90 percent of your time focused on the 10 percent client type.*

So what do these best buyer clients look like? Of all the potential client target groups, how do you distinguish the 10 percent from the other 90 percent? There's a very simple way to filter your list. Identify which ones meet the following three criteria:

Easy. They're readily accessible and easy to reach, costing you little advertising, marketing, and sales effort.

Fast. They have the greatest, most obvious perceived need, so when presented with your solution, they see the value quickly and are quick to make a decision and purchase.

Profitable. They are the type that once converted, their lifetime value is high because of their transaction size, upsell purchases, frequency of repeat purchases, and referrals.

Naturally, there are always fewer best buyers than average buyers. Successfully using this strategy requires you to narrow your target client group. Yes, I said it, *narrow* your list. Focus on fewer people. Tighten up the clients you will serve to the ones you can serve *best*. At first, this can feel wrong, even painful. You'll feel like you're leaving money on the table or ignoring opportunities you can't afford to ignore.

Let me tell you: You can't afford *not* to.

The key to greater profits is rarely capturing more clients.
The key to greater profits is capturing more *valuable* ones.

9. FIND YOUR DREAM 50

Now narrow even further. If a best buyer client can be worth 100 times the average client—and cost you a lot fewer headaches and wallet-aches—what are the "Best of the Best" worth? *A lot.* How do I know? This Dream 50 strategy is the very reason *SUCCESS* magazine is in business.

You may already know that the first issue of *SUCCESS* magazine had a record-breaking launch: over a million copies sold. The biggest first-issue magazine release EVER.

Bigger than Oprah.

Bigger than Martha.

Bigger than all things Condé Nast, which launched a similar

magazine at the exact same time called *Portfolio*. Heard of it? No? That's because it's gone.

While the numbers tell you *what* we accomplished, now I'll share with you *how* we did it.

In March 2008, we re-launched *SUCCESS*—a venerable magazine with a rich history. Originally founded 120 years ago, it was published for decades by various luminaries in the personal development field. Unfortunately, for years prior to our taking the reins, it had *failed*, spectacularly, three times in a row under three previous publishers. The publishing world mocked our beloved magazine with the favored punch line: "*SUCCESS* Fails Again!" Not only that, but in 2008 we were at the forefront of the economic recession, and magazine ad revenue plummeted more than 50 percent—all this right at the time when many claimed print was dead! "Paper is extinct—Long live digital!" could be heard from the rooftops of many a New York City skyscraper, as print operations braced themselves for certain Armageddon.

From the outside looking in, we weren't launching a magazine. We were digging a grave—our own.

From the *inside*, the view wasn't much better. We had spent every dollar we had on acquisition, development, and production. I remember looking at the budget and seeing a big, fat ZERO in the "Marketing" column. We had a magazine, yes, but we had absolutely no conventional way of telling people about it.

Under these dire circumstances, we implemented the Dream 50 strategy. With the content complete and the pages in final editing, the team at *SUCCESS* got together around a conference table under fluorescent lighting and asked ourselves:

"How can we sell magazines not one by one, but by the tens of thousands?"

"Who do we know who is responsible for large networks of people who yearn to be inspired, empowered, and more successful?"

"Who are the 50 people we need to sell on the idea of a magazine that teaches the secrets of success, a magazine for achievers? Fifty people who, if they believed, could bring us *millions*?"

Once we had our list of 50, we focused all of our time and energy on selling them (and *only* them) on *SUCCESS*, on what we stood for, and on what we could do for our readers.

That Dream 50 made our dreams come true.

From a modest conference room in Lake Dallas, Texas (not exactly the epicenter of publishing, media, or… well, anything, really), that list of 50 people was all it took to outsell the other publishing behemoths. Instead of focusing on the million individuals we wanted to reach (expensive, time-consuming, and not likely), we focused on a few key relationships that could connect us to the rest.

In fact, not all 50 engaged. Not even *half* of them did. Candidly, *SUCCESS* broke a multi-decade losing streak with the help of eight believers. Just eight people who saw the vision and got on board.

While I am extremely proud of the one million copies sold of that first issue and humbled by the many millions that have been sold since, the bigger lesson here is this: Think of what *your* Dream 50 can do. You want to turn your roller coaster into a rocket ship? Here's how you do it.

If you could build a dream list, who would be on it? Narrow the universe of available prospects down to that best of the best. Often, your Dream 50 will consist of people you don't currently even have on your prospect list. You might not have had the courage to write them down before. Add them now! Make a Big Kahunas list—those you dream of being in business with. These are prospects who, with just one or two converted to clients, could change your world and the future of your family.

Since you've made it this far, congrats! By now there should be no doubt in your mind that the only fuel you need to make this ride race forward at speeds that defy gravity is one word: *sales*! Your entire business starts, is sustained by, and ends with sales.

"You are one or two dream clients away from changing your future. Go get 'em!"

@DarrenHardy #JoinTheRide

Stop hiding and start selling. You know not to put your prospects on a "hit list" but to climb in bed with them instead (metaphorically, of course!) so you can feel how they feel and help them solve the problems that keep them up at night. Talk less, listen more, build bridges, and don't be afraid to shock and awe your way to the top!

ACTION PLAN

GO TO THE RESOURCE PAGE AND COMPLETE THE WORKSHEETS ON:

- Assessing your current strategic priority

- Building a step-by-step strategic plan to capture your own Dream 50 and shock and awe campaign

Go to: RollerCoasterBook.com/Resources

If each of us hires people who are smaller than we are, we shall become a company of dwarfs. But if each of us hires people who are bigger than we are, we shall become a company of giants.

—David Ogilvy, CEO of Ogilvy & Mather

CHAPTER 4
FILLING YOUR EMPTY SEATS

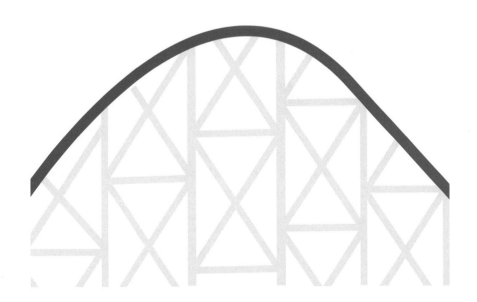

FIND THE BEST OR DIE WITH THE REST (YOUR CHOICE)

Shortly after publishing *The Compound Effect,* things started to get a little crazy. Not only was I on an endless media whistle-stop tour promoting the new book and its message, I was also managing all of the responsibilities of my role as publisher of *SUCCESS* magazine. I was keynoting conferences all over the world, being interviewed constantly, and burning through six tubes of travel-sized toothpaste a month.

And although in this whirlwind called my life, I still never forgot an anniversary or birthday, I was just a few calendar alerts away from an implosion. There was no question—I needed to hire someone.

So I did what any *desperately-seeking-employee freak* does: I posted an ad on Craigslist.

"Rock Star Executive Assistant Wanted: Looking for something fun, flexible, fast-paced, working on projects that make a significant positive difference in people's lives? If so, you have found your dream opportunity!"

Within a few hours of clicking "Post," I received hundreds of responses. Some were strange ("Is there a graveyard shift available?") and some completely crazy ("I have no experience in office managing, but I can crochet coffee cup sleeves for you."). But amidst the madness, one person did stand out—Amanda. Her email was witty, and without even looking at her résumé, I had a good feeling about her. I invited her to interview for the position that same day and was not disappointed.

From the moment she sat down, I knew I liked her. She was fun and funny. She was a long-time *SUCCESS* magazine subscriber, and she had read *The Compound Effect* four times. She even brought her highlighted, underlined, and dog-eared copy to show me. She read the same blogs I did, was familiar with the authors we feature in *SUCCESS*, and she said Jim Rohn reminded her of her grandfather (me, too!). As she held out her *Living Your Best Year Ever* book for me to sign, I couldn't help but fall in professional-love with Amanda.

Moments later, I signed her book: *You're hired!* She read it and her eyes watered up. I said: "Starting tomorrow!" We hugged. Not professional, I know, but it was *that* right.

I went home that night relieved that finding the perfect person had been so easy and the process was over. I could just delete the other several hundred responses that continued to pour in.

The next morning Amanda showed up at my office and got to work.

Well, she *kind of* got to work.

There was a lot of handholding in those first few days. A lot of walking Amanda through basic procedures—and then walking her through them again an hour later. And then again. And one more time… before lunch.

I didn't concern myself with it too much at first. I mean, there is a learning curve with all new jobs, right? She was clearly the perfect person to have on my team—we were so aligned in our beliefs and interests, how could it not work?

As the weeks went on, I continued to give Amanda latitude because I liked her so much—or rather, I liked how much she liked *me* and what I was trying to accomplish. However, as *employing* Amanda became more work than *not* employing Amanda, I became suspicious that something wasn't right.

During a dinner party I mentioned my conundrum to my sister-in-law Laura. Laura was the high-level assistant to a C-level executive of a major pharmaceutical company. I told her how perfect Amanda was for the job and inquired how long it typically takes to get up to speed with the kind of work I was asking her to do. Laura was kind enough to offer to meet with Amanda to give her some pointers and perhaps provide me with more insight into the situation.

After her lunch with Laura, Amanda returned to the office, gushing as usual: "Laura was so sweet! Laura was so smart! Laura was such an inspiration!" It was music to my ears. *Great news!* I thought. It looked like Amanda was as perfect for the job as I had thought.

That evening I got a call from my beloved sister-in-law.

"What were you *thinking*?" she said when I picked up the phone.

"Huh?" was all I could say. I was shocked! I managed to stammer that Amanda said the meeting went great.

"Darren. Did you even *look* at her résumé?"

My silence was clearly answer enough, and she kept right on going. "You told me that you needed someone proficient in Photoshop and who was tech-savvy enough to manage the back end of WordPress. You told me you needed someone who understood the ecology of social media and who could, at the very least, use Google Docs. Darren, Amanda doesn't even know what a Google Doc *is*, and she's been working for you for a month!"

I was still speechless.

Exasperated, she continued: "I really don't know what made you think she would be a good fit—she has none of the skills you need. Not. One."

Immediately, I understood where Laura's confusion was coming from—she couldn't see the little love triangle between Amanda, my ego, and me. All Laura saw was an unqualified candidate, and that was clearly something my starry-eyed "she believes in what I'm doing" vision couldn't discern.

Truly wanting to help (and seeing that I needed it), Laura offered to do the next round of hiring. She reviewed the applicants as they came in, chose her favorite three, and after interviewing them together, highly recommended one: Maggie.

"Maggie?" I couldn't believe she chose Maggie. I mean, Maggie was fine. There was nothing wrong with Maggie. She seemed competent, responsible, capable, but she didn't light my hair on fire. She wasn't a subscriber to *SUCCESS* magazine and didn't seem to even recognize the name John C. Maxwell.

Truthfully, I was a little underwhelmed. I was expecting fireworks, like with Amanda. Employee-love-at-first-sight sparks. There were none. Nevertheless, I decided to follow my sister-in-law's strong suggestion (partly because I trusted her and partly because I knew Georgia would kill me if Laura went through all of that trouble just to have me ignore her advice in the end).

I hired Maggie.

And let me tell you.

I love Maggie!

She is A-M-A-Z-I-N-G!!

Maggie is a freaking rock star at what she does. Maggie has been working for me for years now, and every time we take on a new project or expand in a new direction, Maggie is right there keeping everything running smoothly. Now I can't imagine my life *without* Maggie. Far better than simply gushing about the dream, Maggie has the skills to truly impact making the dreams come true.

One of the fastest (and most common) ways to derail your roller coaster car and send it to a fiery death is to hire and keep the wrong people. Conversely, the only way to dominate your industry, accomplish your grand mission, and "dent the universe," as Steve Jobs said, is to learn how to recruit, keep, and draw the best out of top talent. In this chapter, you will learn to do just that.

"Entrepreneurs are hopeless romantics. Which makes us terrible hiring managers. Get help!"

@DarrenHardy #JoinTheRide

THE ENTREPRENEUR'S DILEMMA

No matter who you are, or how big your company is (or isn't), there is nothing easy about finding the perfect people to join you on this ride. And unfortunately for us entrepreneurs, it's even harder. We are

125

notoriously terrible at hiring people. Truly awful.

Why? Because we are hopeless romantics. If someone shows just a little love for our idea, our hearts start beating faster and stars glitter in our eyes. If someone shows belief in our grand plan, we want to believe in *them*. We are major suckers for someone, *anyone*, who shows enthusiasm for our cause or compliments us on our shoes.

Entrepreneurs see the potential in everything and everyone, and we are happy to hire on hope alone. And while this unique optimism is one of our greatest strengths, when it comes to hiring, we're more vulnerable than poor Achilles with his bum heel.

An entrepreneur cannot hire on hope alone.

When it comes to recruiting and hiring people to occupy a seat on your roller coaster, you can't hire *enthusiasm*. You need to hire *evidence*. You do not have the time or the resources to train or develop anyone's skill or attitude. Trust me, you've got too many other things going on! You simply need to go recruit people who *already have*, by *evidence*, what you need and then place them into your organization.

This means being extremely rational and pragmatic (two words that probably don't appear in the entrepreneurial version of Webster's). You will need to set up a recruiting and hiring process to protect yourself from yourself, and stay committed to it no matter who tells you they "really think you're on to something."

Write this on a sticky and put it on your computer screen:

Hire evidence, not hope.

Now keep reading. The rest of this chapter will teach you how.

THE COSTLIEST MISTAKES YOU CAN MAKE

If your business has employees already, then you'll be more than familiar with the following stat. If you don't yet have a payroll, brace yourself:

The average business has about 65 to 80 percent of its operating costs consumed by salaries and wages.

That's an awful big slice of the overhead pie. Huge.

However, as bold (read: frightening) as that statistic is, the true depth of payroll expense cannot be measured in "hours-in/dollars-out" terms. That would be misleading and far too simple. There is a secret, unspoken dark side to company payrolls that many don't understand or even know exists until it's too late and their company folds because of it.

What is this crippling overhead expense? It's the unofficial price tag that comes with poor hiring choices—and poor includes the good, the bad, and the ugly employees. Here is the truth about each of them:

The Good: You want good people on your team, right? Wrong! A *typical* "good" employee only works at about *half* capacity. By the time you factor in water cooler chitchat, Internet, email, personal business, and a thousand other daily distractions, half capacity might even be optimistic. The average "good" employee simply isn't all that productive.

The Bad: Merely one step below the "good" employees, things get much worse. Unwilling, disengaged employees destroy morale, make costly mistakes, alienate customers, and have all the productivity of road kill. These employees will cost you *much* more in intangible damages than the hourly wage you already pay them.

The Ugly: When I say "ugly," I'm not talking about poor fashion or bad dental work. I'm talking about the actual financial costs of hiring the wrong person. If you add up the cost of recruiting, paying, training, maintaining, and severing a poorly performing employee, along with his or her mistakes, missed opportunities, and failures, the average cost of a bad hire is about *6 to 15 times* the person's annual salary.

"By keeping bad employees, you are cutting them a check to make you broke and miserable."

@DarrenHardy #JoinTheRide

Bottom line: Good employees are barely productive, and bad employees… well, you're just cutting them a check for making you broke and

127

miserable. This is no exaggeration! Do the math—at the very least, even for an entry-level, minimum-wage job, you're going to pay *six figures* as a penalty for a bad hire. And for positions higher up the food chain? Scary. Here's the frightening reality: When you hire the wrong person, you're not only paying them, *you're paying them to light piles of your money on fire, spread a cancer throughout your building, and run your roller coaster right off the tracks and into the ground.*

Do I have your attention? Will you make time and give focus to recruiting and hiring the right people? I hope so. This is a lesson that took me a while to learn, and it cost me dearly. But I learned it.

I *still* hate the process. It's my least favorite thing to do. But I give it serious time, attention, and focus because it's the most significant determinant in whether we will accomplish our mission or not. Whether we will win or not. Whether humanity is advanced and the universe feels our dent or not.

When it comes to filling your roller coaster ride with people, good isn't good enough. Your only option is to hire *great* people or you're going to get vomited on during the very first hairpin turn. Blech.

A-PLAYERS ONLY

Let's talk for a moment about this mysterious creature called the "great employee."

This legendary unicorn wandering among endless fields of regular old pony-employees is reputed to have mysterious powers. Just one *great* hire, one "A-player" unicorn, the legend says, can replace three good ones (and an infinite number of lousy ones).

Guess what? The legend is true. Great employees truly are incredible, and they make your life easier and your business better in every way.

Think of when you felt most excited and in control of your business. When you couldn't wait to get to work. Those are the high points of the entrepreneur roller coaster, when the cart is at the top of the summit and for a moment it pauses so you can take in the view laid out before you like a great tapestry. It's awe-inspiring. It's what we live for. It's the pinnacle feeling as an entrepreneur.

Wouldn't you like to spend time there every day?

Great employees can deliver that. They can set you free. Free from that crushing administrative paperwork. Free from the things you aren't good at. Free from the things you hate. Free from the daily "emergencies" and decisions that shouldn't consume your days, but always seem to.

Great people are what pull you out of the screaming dives and blind corners and crushing gravity of the entrepreneur roller coaster. No technology, productivity strategy, or Big Kahuna partner can consistently deliver what a great employee can.

No, "A-players" aren't mythical unicorns. They really do exist. And they're not just *better* than the good "B-players" and lousy "C-players." They're the *opposite* of them.

Here's why:

1. A-PLAYERS ARE A-PLAYER MAGNETS

A-players want to work with other A-players! This is why organizations like Apple, Google, Virgin, and the like continue to attract A-players. A-players want to work where other A-players work. It's a self-perpetuating attraction mechanism, but only if you monitor and protect it closely.

"A-players hire A-players, and B-players hire C-players. We only want 'A' players here."

—Steve Jobs #JoinTheRide

As Steve Jobs said, "A-players hire A-players, and B-players hire C-players. We only want A-players here."

Otherwise, you get what he called "the Bozo explosion." A-players won't work for a B-player, and B-players don't want to hire an A-player out of protection for their jobs—they pick C's to make themselves look better. As soon as you hire a B-player, the Bozo factor starts to skyrocket. Before you know it, you're running a circus of jealousy, backbiting, and drama.

Your people are your most important recruiting tool. Get an A-player on board, then have them call all their A-player friends. Promote your A-player to the world of other A-players looking to join an A-team. A-players are like a vaccine for the mediocrity virus, and the more A-players you *have*, the more A-players you'll *find*.

2. A-PLAYERS WIN

Remember my real estate agent John Lennon? Like many business owners, he was competing in an industry where the products are essentially the same. But he was *miles* ahead of the competition. I see the same thing everywhere: Even when everyone's selling identical products, there are winners and losers. There's always a market leader, and there's always someone teetering on the brink of bankruptcy. It all comes down to the quality of your people.

As Sir Richard Branson said,

"A company consists of one thing, really. If I buy a plane from Boeing, it'll be exactly the same plane that BA [British Airways] will buy, which will be exactly the same plane that United [Airlines] will buy, exactly the same plane that Air Canada will buy. So, what is a company? A company is the people that are working inside that plane, the people that are working on the ground. They're the people that make up a company. They either make this company exceptional or average... "

Businesses are not profit and loss statements or balance sheets. They're not systems and processes, tactics and strategies, tasks and deliverables. Businesses are people. Give ten companies the same products, and there will always be a number one and a number ten. Because *it's not about the products*. It's about the people behind them.

As the legendary former CEO of General Electric, Jack Welch, recently said to me in an interview, "The one thing that hasn't changed is the team that fields the best players wins."

"The one thing that hasn't changed is the team that fields the best players wins."

@Jack_Welch #JoinTheRide

3. A-PLAYERS ARE FREE

You might be thinking you can't afford to hire A-players. Who can afford that kind of talent, right?

I've got good news: they're free! That's right, F-R-E-E. Because A-players pay for themselves.

Would you pay someone $250,000 a year in salary and bonuses? You would if they brought in an added $5 million to your business. You'd be *underpaying* them in fact. Would you pay someone $3 million in annual income? With great pleasure and enthusiasm, if they helped you grow another $100 million in revenue. Those are the kinds of results the right A-players can deliver. You just need to ensure you provide them the right opportunities with the right focus and offer the right support.

A CEO from one of my private mentorship forums finally came to this realization:

"The idea that 'great people are free' has changed my business. In the past I was very reluctant to hire people with salaries above $125,000. After this advice, I hired a very talented (and expensive) President for my company. As a result, revenue increased three times in two years (from $60M in revenue to $180M) and more importantly my stress level is 50 percent of what it was because I share that with him. Not to mention that the company could now run without me if needed."

If your business has something worthwhile to offer the market-place, you can always afford to hire A-players—they're free. But B- and C-players? They're very costly, in so many ways. Not only can you afford

A-players, you can't afford *not* to hire them.

Whenever I ask top business leaders what they attribute the success of their businesses to, invariably they say it's the great team of people they have surrounded themselves with. This is not some self-effacing answer. Great leaders know that businesses are nothing but a group of people brought together to accomplish a mission. The better the people, the better chance you have of accomplishing the mission. No CEO climbs to the top of the mountain alone—it requires a great team. Many of these extraordinary achievers will readily confess that most of their team is smarter, more talented, and more skilled than they are. In fact, they will tell you that is always their objective in hiring.

Think about it. You're sitting in the very first car of this roller coaster with a whole train of people—your team—sitting in cars behind you as your ride slowly clicks upward. Then, at the very top of that first summit, there is that subtle pause before the whole thing plummets downward at heart-stopping speeds.

You know it's coming. You know things are about to get crazy.

In that moment, would you rather:

Look back at your team and see them huddled up, closing their eyes, and cowering in fear?

Or...

Look back at your team and see their arms in the air, screams of excitement on their faces, ready to take on this wild ride and enjoy it?

I know which one I would choose.

BUILDING A HIGH-PERFORMANCE CULTURE

We hear a lot about building a great company culture. Let me shortcut this for you: *You cannot shape or create the culture.* The culture of an organization is not a whiteboard exercise done with executives sitting around a conference table spit-balling ideas. The culture of an organization evolves around the people who make up the company.

The culture is the personality and character expression of the people in it. The only way to shape that culture is to focus on hiring people with the attributes you want your culture to have.

Do you want a culture of positive expectation where everyone has a can-do attitude? You need to hire positive, can-do people and remove the people who don't have those qualities. Do you want your culture to be fast-paced, with high energy and have a great sense of urgency? You'll need to hire people who thrive in a fast-paced, high-energy environment with demanding deadlines.

"To have a high-performance culture, you need to hire and maintain high-performing people."

@DarrenHardy #JoinTheRide

To have a high-performance culture, you need to hire and maintain high-performing people. Fill the seats of your roller coaster with people who possess the attributes you want for your culture. It's as simple as that.

Don't settle. It will corrupt your culture and drain the fun—and profit—from your ride.

RECRUITING: YOUR KEY SKILL

If you're saying to yourself, "But I don't like to recruit" or, "I'll just hire someone to do the recruiting," let me stop that thought right now.

When your company expands beyond just you—and it will need to if it hasn't already—the choices you make in the recruiting process are, in effect, determining your future. Just one person can make the difference. Do it right, and one great hire can set you free. Rush it, do it on the cheap, get lazy, become fearful, ignore warning signs, or have someone else do it for you, and you're going to ride this coaster right off the rails to certain disaster. Sure, you can have someone lead the process (like Laura did for me), but you still need to be the final interview, the final stamp of approval or the final veto.

Put it this way: The quality of your life and your ability to fulfill your mission come down to the process you will develop and the choices you will make about who you do and don't allow aboard your roller coaster. I'm not kidding—these are life or death choices for your entrepreneurial dreams. Learn masterfully and choose carefully.

"The single most important thing you need to do is pick the right people and keep them. There is NOTHING more important than this."

—Jim Collins #JoinTheRide

As Jim Collins, author of *Good to Great*, said, "The single most important thing you need to do is pick the right people and keep them. There is NOTHING more important than this."

> Want to double your business? It starts with hiring right.
> Want to reduce your stress? It starts with hiring right.
> Want to dominate your market?
> Yep. It starts with hiring right.

Selection, my fellow coaster-rider, is 95 percent of success.

The best news is that *this is completely within your control.* This is your company and your dream. You get to decide. And as you'll see, you don't need to have a big brand, deep pockets, or a volleyball court in your lobby to attract great people. What you do need is a simple set of principles to keep this roller coaster on the rails as you start to add people to the ride.

BE A MASTER RECRUITER: THREE PRINCIPLES
PRINCIPLE 1: KNOW WHAT YOU WANT

It's one thing to preach the importance of people. But it's another thing entirely to know what that means.

What does the "right" person for your business look like? What distinguishes great from plain old "good"? How do you tell the As from the Bs and Cs?

An A-player in your business will meet these three criteria:

1. THEY ARE BETTER THAN YOU.

Georgia and I were in Barcelona, Spain, and spent the afternoon with an extremely successful CEO and his wife. The more time I spent with him, though, the more I couldn't believe he was CEO of anything, never mind a multibillion-dollar telecom. He was a bit scatterbrained, chewed with his mouth open, and laughed too loudly and too long at his not-so-appropriate (or funny) jokes. I just couldn't understand it.

Finally, I managed to tactfully ask him (removing as much skepticism as possible from my tone) how he'd managed to become so successful.

"Your goal is to be the dumbest one in the room. Hire people BETTER than you."

@DarrenHardy #JoinTheRide

His answer? "My goal is to always be the dumbest one in the room."

What? The *dumbest* one? Isn't the CEO supposed to be the *smartest*?

As he explained to me, it wasn't his intelligence, sophistication, charisma, or motivational abilities that made him so successful. (Trust me, it wasn't.) It was simply the discipline of always having the smartest and best people in every chair around his leadership table.

"If I am in a meeting with my leadership team and we are discussing a marketing opportunity," he said, "if I have a better idea than my marketing director, we are in trouble. If I solve a problem my CFO has been stumped with for a week, we are doomed. If I have an operational efficiency solution my COO hasn't thought of, it's the beginning of the end. I always hire the best possible people for every chair at my table. Then *they* deliver the great performance."

His sole job was to get them to the table so they could deliver.

And it's your job, too.

2. THEY HAVE THE CHARACTER.

Several years ago I had the opportunity to have lunch with the chairman of Marriott International.

Marriott has a reputation for amazing customer service. Stories abound of Marriott employees going above and beyond the call of duty to deliver extraordinary levels of customer care. I had stayed the night before at one of the Marriott properties, and the approach was evident everywhere. Every Marriott person I encountered, from the front desk manager and the concierge to the room-service delivery person seemed so personable. Not the over-the-top, cheesy, butt-kissing, the-customer-is-always-right kind of "nice," but genuinely *friendly*.

After so many positive interactions, the first words out of my mouth when I shook the chairman's hand the next morning were, "It's incredible. You have to tell me what you do to train your people to be so friendly."

"You don't train your people to be successful. You hire successful people."

@DarrenHardy #JoinTheRide

He seemed puzzled then replied matter-of-factly. "We don't train our people to be friendly," he said. "We just hire friendly people."

We just hire friendly people. Five words. Those five words woke me up to one of the greatest recruiting keys I've ever discovered. So many businesses struggle with even the *basics* of good service, and on the surface it looks like a training problem. But in truth, that assumption couldn't be more wrong; you *can't* train people to be friendly. They either are or they aren't.

You can't train for character. You can't teach people to be disciplined, hardworking, consistent, loyal, positive, friendly, or whatever trait is most important to you. You can only commit to hiring people who *already* have those attributes. As Roy Williams, the Basketball Hall of Fame head coach of the University of North Carolina, once said, "I recruit character as much as I recruit ability."

Want a "suggested attribute list"? Here's what Warren Buffett looks for: integrity, intelligence, and energy. And he warns that if they don't have that first quality, the others will work against you—that if you hire an intelligent, energetic person who lacks integrity, it'll kill you and your business. "If you *do* hire someone without the first [integrity], hope they are dumb and lazy," quips Buffett.

What attributes do you want? Do you want someone passionate? Persistent? Bold? Reliable, consistent, hardworking?

What do you want?

Sit down. Make a list. And start looking.

If you don't know what you want, you can't find it!

3. THEY ARE IN LOVE.

Steve Jobs said, "When I hire somebody really senior, competence is the ante. They have to be really smart. But the real issue for me is, *Are they going to fall in love with Apple?* Because if they fall in love with Apple, everything else will take care of itself. They'll want to do what's best for Apple, not what's best for them, what's best for Steve, or anybody else."

My mistake with Amanda was not setting competency as the first gate to pass through. But once you cross that bridge, it's time to look beyond the résumé.

When you're sitting across the interview table with someone, don't just look at their résumé; look into their eyes. Look deep into their heart. Ask yourself, *Is this the kind of person who could fall in love with what we do here? Do they have the personality, attitude, passion, and heart for the work we do?*

If the answer is yes, then ask yourself, *Would they thrive in our company's culture? Would our work environment feel like their natural habitat?* A great person in the wrong environment is still the wrong person.

One of the most admired company cultures in the country is run by our 2013 *SUCCESS* Achiever of the Year, Tony Hsieh, CEO of Zappos. If you take a tour of their offices (offered daily), you will see one of the zaniest, wildest, and, well, weirdest office environments you've ever experienced. If I were being considered for a job there, while I believe I am quite talented and capable, that environment wouldn't work for me. It's just not "me." I'm not of that personality. I'd fail in that cultural environment. I'd be the right person in the wrong environment (for me), and the wrong person for Zappos to hire.

"The right person in the wrong culture (for them) is the wrong person."

@DarrenHardy #JoinTheRide

You have to evaluate people with a yardstick that goes beyond their résumé and looks to their heart, character, and personality type. They need to be the kind of person who can fall in love with your culture, your people, your products, and your mission.

If they can, then as Jobs promised, "Everything else will take care of itself."

PRINCIPLE 2: KNOW WHAT THEY WANT

If you've read this far and a voice in your head keeps repeating over and over again, "I still don't think I can afford A-players," then what I'm about to say next is for you. Are you ready? Pay close attention—this is important:

People don't want what you think they want.

Really. They don't. If you're worried about "affording A-players" as far as the payroll is concerned, you've got this thing all wrong. Here's what you're missing: In the same way entrepreneurs like you are reinventing what it means to be in business, *employees* are looking at work and careers in a whole new way, too.

This is really exciting stuff. You'll never look at recruiting the same way. Here, according to Brad Smart's *Topgrading* book, are the five things employees are looking for in the workplace.

1. PEOPLE.

As we've already discussed, great people join the Googles and Apples of the world in droves not because of the dental coverage, but because *that's where all the other great people are*. Great people want to work with great people. It's self-perpetuating. It's the number one thing people are looking for.

2. CHALLENGE.

Great people want to be a part of something great. They want work that excites and fulfills them. They want work with intrinsic value, not just work for the sake of work. Actor-turned-producer Hugh Jackman graced our *SUCCESS* cover in August 2013 and put it this way: "Quality talent is attracted to the extraordinary challenge that's presented. Don't just dangle the prospect of a good job; tempt them with the prospect of quality work. There's a difference, and it will dictate the talent you attract." Each night, great people want to climb into bed feeling exhausted yet satisfied by the great work they did that day.

3. OPPORTUNITY.

Great people want the opportunity to move up. They need an upside, something to grow into. They want to know you are an organization on the go, with your sights set on big goals, ambitions, and expansion plans. Additionally, they don't want to be a spectator—great people want to participate in company progress, to help "make it happen." As Steve Jobs said, "People are attracted to vision. 'Put a dent in the universe' attracted like-minded people who shared that vision. That became our advantage."

4. GROWTH.

People have finally realized that the job they pick is going to take up two-thirds of their waking hours. They want to feel good about what they do, but they also want to know they are going to grow, develop, and become more of who they want to *be*. They want to be with organizations that invest in the growth and development of their people. My mentor Jim Rohn said, "Learn to help people with more than just their jobs; learn to help people with their *lives*." If you can develop the reputation of being a company that cares about people's lives, you will have more great people knocking on your door than you'll know what to do with.

5. MONEY.

And, of course, great people want to be paid well for delivering great work.

"Money is not the primary motivator for an A-player. Don't just recruit with a paycheck."

@DarrenHardy #JoinTheRide

Notice what's most important about this list? *Money is at the bottom*! That's right. Money is not the primary motivator for an A-player. It's not even in the top three! They want to work with other great people, doing something challenging and meaningful that enables them to grow in every way. They'll take a job that gives them great work with great people over a crappy job with great pay.

So how does *your* current recruiting script read? Maybe backward? Are you advertising a salary and a job description blah, blah, blah? If so, my guess is you're getting "blah, blah, blah" kinds of applicants. It's time to change things up and adjust your strategy.

If you're soliciting applicants to fill one of the exclusive seats on your ride, the headline should talk about the opportunity to work with other extremely talented, fun, passionate, and high-character people who are fired up about the great mission, challenge, and vision you are trying to realize. Explain how you invest in your people to help them grow, develop, and achieve their goals—professionally and personally. Then (maybe) footnote the compensation package.

Personally I never even list the compensation plan. I always just say, "much better than market standard." That's it. No mention of numbers, no list of the typical benefits. I just make it clear that if they're the right person, I'll pay them well.

And I do. I always pay better than market standard. Why?

Because great people are free, remember?

If you want an A-level company, and you're worried about being able to afford it, it's time to change your thinking. If you truly want an A-level company, you can't *afford* to hire B-level players. Always be willing to pay for the best.

PRINCIPLE 3: THE F-FACTOR

I recently hosted an elite mastermind event in South Beach, Miami; and when I say elite, I mean *very* exclusive. Only 28 invitations were extended to a group of the greatest, most innovative minds in business today.

While we dined on prosciutto-wrapped scallops on a mega-yacht under the stars with a view of the Miami skyline, I had a deep conversation with one of my invited guests, Cody Foster.

Cody is one of the co-founders of the multibillion-dollar enterprise Advisors Excel. (Yes, I said *billion*, and yes, I said *multi*.) He and his team crush the competition in their market space, and they do all of this domination from their office in the booming metropolis of…

Topeka, Kansas. Not what you think of when you think multibillion, perhaps, but Cody and his company are wildly successful.

As Cody stepped on to the yacht that night, I noticed that he was sporting a tan that didn't seem to fit my picture of mid-winter Topekans. When I teased him about it, he chuckled. No, he hadn't been to a tanning booth. He had arrived from his company trip in Cancun, Mexico.

141

"Every year," he said, "We set what we call a Stretch Goal—a sales goal that is pretty big, but attainable. If we hit it, we take them to Cancun. Flight, room, food… we cover it all."

"Nice!" I said. "That's a great trip for your sales producers."

"No, no," he said. "It's not just the sales team. It's everyone."

"*Everyone?!*" I nearly choked on my scallop.

"Well," he paused to correct himself. "Everyone and a guest."

I began quickly doing the mental math. I knew his company employed about 250 people from top to bottom. Double that if everyone brought a guest, and Cody was flying nearly half the town of Topeka to Mexico every year. I asked him if that was even *possible*—were there enough flights from Topeka to Cancun?

"We charter a few planes," he said. "It's pretty cool actually to be in an airport that's filled with people and every one of them is 'your people.' "

"Wow!" I shook my head, impressed. "No wonder your business is exploding! Who wouldn't want to work somewhere that not only gives you vacation days, but gives you a full-fledged *vacation*!"

Cody looked at me for a moment, and I had the distinct sense that I was missing something. I could see him thinking, considering how best to phrase what he was about to say next.

"Well. Yes. The Mexico trip is really fun, but Mexico itself isn't what makes our company a fun place to work. It's what happens in the process of winning the trip that matters. "

By now, a small group had gathered, and Cody continued. "From the very first day, new employees know that a lot is expected of them. They know that, between the hours of eight and five, they are giving everything they've got to the job they were hired to do. Whether they are a receptionist, in operations, or working in the compliance department, it's critical that they are looking for ways to connect with the clients, to find better ways of serving them, to build relationships.

"We're not the kind of office with ping-pong tables or 'bring your dog to work' days or themed happy hours every Friday. And Mexico isn't enough. What makes work *fun* is doing meaningful work."

What makes work fun is doing meaningful work. The words echoed in my mind, and I resisted the urge to start scribbling notes on my appetizer napkin. Cody continued, "Mexico or no Mexico, even if we didn't do the 'fun stuff,' people would still want to work here... because every day, it's just a fun place to be."

"What makes work fun is doing meaningful work."

@CodyGFoster #JoinTheRide

Throughout this hiring process, you have to remember you are recruiting humans. Humans like to have fun. Humans like to love what they are doing. They know they're going to spend two-thirds of their life working. It can't be drudgery or just "putting in the time" as if they have a prison sentence. Their work, their life (the two-thirds you influence) has to be fun, meaningful, and rewarding.

Cody's business, Advisors Excel, isn't a fun place to work *because* of a great trip. A great trip evolved from his company being a fun place to work.

No one knows this third principle of recruiting great people better than Sir Richard Branson. He is the unofficial king of fun, and Branson agrees, "Business should be fun. Creating an exciting work culture is the best way to motivate and retain good people. It also means you don't have to pay them as much. More than any other element, fun is the secret to Virgin's success."

But Branson doesn't just *talk* about fun. It's a guiding principle for how he lives and what opportunities he takes on. "I can honestly say that I have never gone into any business purely to make money," he says. "If that is the sole motive, then I believe you are better off not doing it. A business has to be involving, it has to be fun."

That's the F-Factor.

Is your business involving? Do the people who work for you look forward to coming to the office for eight hours every weekday? Does their work *mean* something to them? If not, it's time to put on your party hat and make some changes because there's nothing more eerie than a roller coaster in motion with no one on the ride.

143

I know that recruiting can seem daunting. I know that there are many, many more B- and C-player applications coming in for every *one* A-player résumé you read, and if you really need to hire someone pronto, it might be tempting to settle instead of holding out for the perfect match. But just like you would tell your daughter who is thinking of marrying a C-player-kind-of-guy, trust me when I say *the right one is worth the wait*.

PUTTING OUT THE FIRE WITH GASOLINE

If I haven't made it abundantly clear by now, then here it is again: Your business will only be as good as the people you recruit to join it. Your future and the future of your business depend on your ability to recruit without compromise.

"Your business will only be as good as the people you recruit to join it."

@DarrenHardy #JoinTheRide

Remember this: The bigger your dream, the more important your team. If you have small, unambitious dreams, then you only need a small, unambitious team. If you have big and extraordinary goals, then you're going to need to sell a big and extraordinary team of people on joining you in order to accomplish them.

Your employees will change everything about your business. *Everything.* They're going to be intimately involved with finding and serving your customers, creating your products, marketing your services, and developing the culture that you and everyone else on your roller coaster spend the vast majority of their time either loving or despising. If you want that change to be positive, you cannot settle for anything less than the best.

The single biggest mistake I see entrepreneurs make when growing their teams is seeing hiring as a solution to a problem—they hire to put out fires.

Don't.

Hire ahead of your growth. Hire to conquer new frontiers. Hire to launch new initiatives. But don't hire to put out a fire.

Because the first thing you grab might be a bucket of gasoline.

Be smart. Be strategic. Be proactive. And be patient. Only hire the best. And once you load all those great people onto the roller coaster and buckle them in, what happens next?

Look carefully. There's only one seat left on the roller coaster. It's the scariest place to sit but also the most exhilarating. It's the front seat. And it's yours.

You've got the people. Now it's time to lead them.

ENTREPRENEUR

ACTION PLAN

GO TO THE RESOURCE PAGE AND COMPLETE THE WORKSHEETS ON:

- Assessing the competency, skill, and dedication of the top five positions in your company and the people occupying those positions now

- Designing your A-players: What you're looking for in skills, competencies, and character and how success will be measured

- Designing your offer, job postings, and recruiting scripts

Go to: RollerCoasterBook.com/Resources

Leadership is the ability to get extraordinary achievement from ordinary people.

—Brian Tracy

CHAPTER 5

RIDING IN THE FRONT SEAT

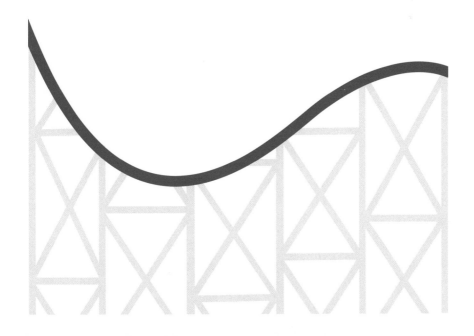

LEADERSHIP: STEPPING UP WITHOUT SCREWING UP

Have you ever flown into Las Vegas?

I think the first time is the same for everyone. The plane begins to make its initial descent, and you look out the window expecting neon lights, exotic buildings, and people dangling from the sky on streams of Cirque fabric.

Instead, you see nothing but miles upon miles of rows upon rows of *houses*, all in various shades of desert brown and each one with a crystal blue swimming pool.

And all of a sudden it hits you: People *live* here.

On a recent trip, as my plane banked for the final descent to the airport, I was about to get a new perspective on those thousands of homes. I was in town to have lunch with the CEO of a multibillion-dollar company that had built entire cities just like the one I saw from the sky.

I had been looking forward to meeting with this man for a while—as far as I was concerned, he was a success rock star. At the time of our lunch, his company had over 16,000 employees and was growing at breakneck speed. They were building 200 homes a *day*. Can you even imagine that? Give it a try: Picture for a moment one of those large, perfectly planned suburban home developments. An idyllic neighborhood where cul-de-sacs are plentiful and the color-coordinated rooftops stretch endlessly in every direction. Got that image in your head? *Now imagine building that in just 24 hours.* It would be like mobilizing a small army every single day.

As the CEO ordered his lunch, I tried to fathom being at the helm of that kind of growth. I rolled a few of the variables around in my head—the people he had to manage, the surveying and permitting, the multitude and complexity of timelines, the massive capital required. I thought about the challenges, the problems, and the liabilities. Not to mention the volatile nature of the new-construction market. My mind was spinning just *thinking* about everything required to keep a company growing at that pace. There were just so many things that could go wrong. So many constraints.

As I expressed this to the home-development rock star, though, he seemed unfazed. Dismissive even. In his mind, there was only one factor limiting his company's growth: *him.*

"The only constraint of a company's growth and potential," he told me, "is the owner's ambition. I am the constraint. The market, the opportunity, everything is there. It's up to me to set the pace, clear the obstacles, get the resources, and create the conversations to grow the company faster.

"As CEO," he continued, "the most important thing I manage is *myself.* Do that right, and everything else falls into place." (Just to be clear, "falling into place" for this guy meant a billion dollars a year.)

That single conversation forever changed the way I saw Las Vegas, and it forever changed the way I see myself as a leader. Every time I feel that descent into the LAS airport, I look to the window and the sprawling city below. For me, it's no longer a meaningless sea of desert-landscaped homes. It's the expression of a leader's ambition.

And I remind myself: As a leader, *I* am my *only* constraint.

151

> # "The number one bottleneck or constraint to the growth of any organization is the leader."
>
> @DarrenHardy #JoinTheRide

Doing what that CEO did for a company that size takes some serious leadership. But what he said of his organization and its limitations isn't just true of billion-dollar companies—it's true of *any* company, yours included.

The number one bottleneck or constraint to the growth of any organization is the leader.

It's true every time. There are no exceptions. Your leadership ability is the major limit to what you can achieve in business. It's that skill that determines if you can turn this roller coaster into a rocket ship to the moon.

This chapter is about the essentials you need in order to make sure that the *sky*, not your leadership, is the limit.

IT'S YOUR FAULT

Is your company rockin' and rollin'? Are sales high and morale higher? Are you dominating your marketplace and leaving others slack-jawed and mystified? Then go ahead, my leader friend, take a moment to pat yourself on the back and do a little celebration dance. It looks like, at least for now, you're doing a nice job at pushing through your own limitations and, as the leader, you get first dibs on the credit.

Feel good? Okay. Now stop.

Because, yes, while you are "to blame" when things go right…

… when they go wrong, it's also your fault. *All* your fault.

"As the leader, you ultimately have 100% responsibility for everything. Don't waste your time blaming."

@DarrenHardy #JoinTheRide

As the leader, you ultimately have 100 percent responsibility for *everything*. When a widget rolls off the line with a broken thingamajig, it's not the fault of the guy who was texting instead of quality-controlling. It's your fault. When a customer is mistreated at a store halfway across the country, don't blame the customer service agent with a bad attitude. *You're* to blame. Top to bottom, front to back. Everything. Is. Your. Fault.

After all:

When a company gets in trouble, what do they do? They fire the CEO.

When a team starts losing? They replace the head coach.

When the country's not doing well? They want to oust the president!

Sure, when your ship comes in, you're going to win big.

But if the ship goes down? You go down with it, Captain.

THE MATH OF DECEPTION

Knowing that everything hinges on you, there's only one question you should be asking right now: *How's my leadership?*

Let me guess your answer: *I gotta say, Darren, it's pretty good.*

Am I right? Is that your answer?

You think you're at *least* above average? Maybe better?

Are you *sure*?

Studies consistently show that we often think we're better at things than we *really* are. Doctors, pilots, teachers—the vast majority of professionals—think they're better than average. Leaders are no different—in fact, 75 percent of people in leadership positions think they are in the top 10 percent of the field.

See anything wrong with that?

The math doesn't work. We can't all be in the top 10 percent. And to make it worse, if you're like most people, *even as you are reading this sentence,* you're *still* thinking: *Well, that doesn't apply to me. I'm ACTUALLY in the top 10 percent.*

Trust me. We all need to take a close look at our leadership skills. When I first heard these statistics, I thought the same thing you did— they're just talking about other people. In fact, in an effort to prove it to myself, I even took my entire team to a leadership seminar.

We were having a great year, and I was feeling pretty good about our performance. I wanted to take things up a notch and reward the team at the same time—and, although I wouldn't have admitted it then, I wanted to stroke my ego, too. But regardless of motive, we all loaded up in a 40-passenger travel bus one Friday afternoon and took off to a beautiful conference center in Santa Barbara for a two-day retreat.

As part of the first day, the seminar leader guided us through a multiple-choice and short-essay exercise that was designed to be a 360-degree review of each member of the team, including me. He gave us an hour, put on some music, and we each sat and anonymously reported on each other's strengths, weaknesses, and personalities.

Oh, I ate it up! I dug right into the exercise, taking care to offer never-before-considered elements of each of my team's strengths and areas of weakness. I was looking forward to both improving the team and earning a few well-earned kudos for my *stellar* leadership.

At the end of the hour, the leader turned off the music, collected the feedback, reassembled it for each member of the team, and excused us to read and process our reviews in private. We would reconvene in an hour to discuss.

I found a little nook next to a window overlooking the bluffs and the sea, and settled in to gorge myself at the ego buffet.

Oh, boy.

As I worked my way through the first few "strongly agree," "agree," "strongly disagree" responses, I could feel my face growing hot and my palms begin to sweat. The way my team saw me was nothing like how I saw myself. Nothing at all.

Where I thought I was being organized and transparent, they saw me as being too secretive and shortsighted. When I thought I was being inspiring and encouraging, they thought I was being demeaning and a braggart.

I picked up the pace a little, quickly scanning each review, looking for a glimmer of confirmation that I was the leader I *knew* I was—that the first few responses were just a fluke. And there *were* some parts that were very complimentary. But as each page passed, there was no hiding from the truth: *I was not the leader I thought I was.*

I was flabbergasted. At first, I felt betrayed and questioned the results. But there was no way around it. This was the truth like I'd never been willing to see it before.

Ironically, it's moments like this, when we question our leadership, that true leadership emerges. I put the papers down and stared out the window, watching the waves rhythmically touch the shore. Sitting there alone, just moments before we were scheduled to return to the group, I knew I had two choices. I could discount the feedback as nonsense and continue to believe what I believed, thereby preserving my ego. Or I could take it seriously and make a decision to get better.

I have to admit I was tempted by the first option. My ego and I have been friends for a long time, and it would be inconsiderate of me to just throw him under the bus. But then I realized the truth: I had fallen for the same trap as most other leaders. I believed I was better than I actually was.

The only solution, I realized, was to stop believing I was better, and simply *get* better.

THIS AIN'T YOUR DADDY'S LEADERSHIP

The choice I faced that day is the same one you face now. The truth is we can *all* improve our ability to lead.

The challenge is that leadership has changed.

For a long time, leadership was a pretty static idea. The industrial age taught us that organizations were economic entities—"machines" for making money. The priorities for leaders in those days were to develop structures, set controls, and leverage capital as effectively as possible—to, in effect, treat parts of the company, including the people, as parts in the machine.

This was accomplished through pyramids of people arranged in hierarchies who performed a fairly narrow range of tasks within clear guidelines. As a leader, your job was to pour orders into the top of the pyramid machine, and watch the results come out the bottom.

And now?

Fuhgettaboutit.

Things have changed. Not only have the rules of business changed, but also the landscape of *who* you need to lead is radically different.

The millennial generation (those born in the 1980s and 1990s) is the largest generation to enter the workforce in human history. Nurtured through a different era, this generation has a completely different value system. They value self-expression, not compliance. They care about independence, not routine.

If you're having a hard time motivating and leading millennials, you'd better figure it out, and quickly. Millennials will soon represent half the current workforce, and by 2020 they'll hold the majority of leadership positions. Like it or not, they're going to play a star role in how the marketplace works in the future. They will make up both your workforce *and* your competition.

Not only is the workforce younger, its gender makeup has shifted. As unemployment figures fluctuate, there are often more *women* working than *men* (and the number of stay-at-home dads has doubled to over 20 percent). This is a massive shift from the previously male-dominant, top-down, rank-and-file, industrial-age corporate system and culture.

But wait! There's more. Adding to this new complexity is the fact that by 2050, minorities will make up 55 percent of the working-age population. Making them what?

Majorities!

Add it all up, and you'll realize the people you're going to be leading are extremely diverse. Did you know that for the first time in history we're going to have five generations in the workplace at once? When the millennials occupy the majority of leadership positions, not only will there be two generations following them, but their parents *and* grandparents will still be working, too. How's that for a mind-blowing, nerve-racking leadership challenge? You can't be an old-school leader in this new-school workplace and expect to thrive.

ENTER THE 21ST CENTURY LEADER

"Leader" used to be synonymous with "boss" or "manager," but not anymore. A boss leads by authority, fear, and command. "You'll do it because I said so. I'm the boss."

Everyone hates bosses. Don't be a boss.

And managers? They try to incentivize with brass rings, Starbucks gift cards, and the chance to ring the bell. "If you do what I say, I'll give you this."

Managers are wienies. Don't be a manager.

So what *should* you be?

This is clearly not your daddy's leadership, but unfortunately that's all most of us know. Leadership to us is what we saw while growing up. Today we are mindlessly repeating the patterns and behaviors of the models we experienced. We are using twentieth-century leadership skills to try to lead in the twenty-first century... and we wonder why it's not working.

So what do you do?

You change. You *adapt.* You become something new. You become a *Twenty-First-Century Leader.*

Twenty-First-Century Leaders aren't bosses. They're not managers. They're not relics from a bygone era. They're *leaders* in the true sense of the word because they understand and embody the four things that set all great leaders apart.

1. LEADERS SET THE PACE

Here's a secret: People don't go as fast as they *can.* They don't work as hard as they can either. They aren't as disciplined as possible. They aren't as positive-minded or enthusiastic as they can be.

They're only as fast and disciplined and positive as *you* are.

As the leader, you set the pace. You create the standards. It doesn't matter if you're leading salespeople, engineers, or creatives. They will only be as disciplined, driven, focused, and consistent as the person leading them. The speed, quality, and culture of the pack are determined by the leader. That means the most important, but also the most underused and violated, principle of leadership is *lead by example.*

Here's how to set a good one.

"People don't go as fast as they can. They only go as fast as the leader. You set the pace."

@DarrenHardy #JoinTheRide

LEAD FROM THE FRONT

In 1944, the Allied generals gathered to discuss their battle plans for the D-Day invasion of Normandy. After listening to how each general was going to send his soldiers into battle, an angered Dwight D. Eisenhower, the supreme commander, slammed his fist down, stood up, and placed a piece of string in the middle of the table.

"Gentlemen," he said, "do you see this string? This string is like an army. Push it from behind, and it doubles up on itself—you get nowhere. To drive it forward you have to pull it from the front, and it will follow you in perfect order."

We should have learned this valuable leadership lesson in preschool. Do you remember preschool? Those early-education years are when we learned the basic skills of sharing, sitting still for more than a minute, and the classic "our hands are not for hitting."

It's also where we learned to walk in a straight line.

I can still hear sweet Mrs. Morrow's voice as she called, "All right, boys and girls, let's line up!" She would stand at the classroom door, and we'd fall into line behind her. She'd grab the tiny palm of a student, and we would all do the same. Mrs. Morrow would open the classroom door and fearlessly guide us, single file, through the hallways to our destination.

Did Mrs. Morrow stand behind us and shout "GO!"? No.

Did she walk along beside us trying to manage our every move? No.

She walked in front, leading the way, and at every turn she called to us: "Follow me!"

Certainly, the people in your organization are not preschoolers (even if it sometimes seems like they would benefit from a nap), but the leadership principle remains the same: If you want to move your organization forward, you can't just give a speech and say *go*. You only need to say, "Follow me," and make your action your instruction.

> # "To lead, you only need to say 'Follow me.' Make your action your instruction."
>
> @DarrenHardy #JoinTheRide

159

ENTREPRENEUR

DO IT FIRST

Before I ever ask someone to do or be anything, I think of Mahatma Gandhi and the story of "The Little Boy and Sweets." It is such a great example to live up to and delivers an invaluable lesson on the character of leadership.

Coming to see Gandhi, a woman waited in line for more than half a day with her son at her side, in order to have an audience with him. When at last it was her turn to speak to him, the woman said, "Mahatma, please. Tell my son he must stop eating sweets. It is ruining his health, his teeth. It affects his mood. Every time he has sweets, I see the change in him, and there is nothing I can do to stop him from eating more and more. He's a good boy, but when it comes to sweets, he becomes a liar and a thief and a cheat, and I'm afraid it will ruin his life. Please, Mahatma, tell him to stop."

Gandhi looked at the boy for a long moment as he cowered there, trying to hide in his mother's sari. Finally, Gandhi broke the silence and said, "Come back to me in two weeks' time." Confused, and a bit disappointed that he could not simply tell her son to stop eating sugar, the mother left with her son.

Two weeks later the woman returned with her child and once again waited in line for hours before finally it was their turn to see the Master. "Mahatma," said the mother, "we have returned. We came to you for help with this boy and eating sweets, and you asked us to come back after two weeks."

"Yes, of course I remember," said Gandhi. "Come here, child." He motioned the boy forward.

The boy, at the urging and prodding of his mother, disentangled himself from her sari and stepped up to Gandhi, who reached out, put his hands on the boy's shoulders, and pulled him closer. He looked the boy squarely in the eye and said, firmly, "Don't eat sweets." Then he released him.

"That's it?" said the mother. "That's all you're going to say?" She was flabbergasted. "Why didn't you just tell him that two weeks ago?"

"Because," replied Gandhi, "two weeks ago I was still eating sweets myself. I could not ask him to stop eating sweets so long as I had not stopped either."

"Ask only for others to do what you have done yourself first."

@DarrenHardy #JoinTheRide

If you really want to have leadership influence, you have no choice but, as Gandhi, to be the change you want to see in others. Leadership in the twenty-first century is less about the words that come out of you and more about what exists within you. Is there a behavior that is rotting the teeth of your organization and ruining its health? If so, you'll need to be the first one to throw those sweets away.

MONKEY SEE, MONKEY DO

A mother of six who I know is the most affectionate, affirming woman I have ever met. Her children are the purpose of her life. For decades she poured incredible amounts of love and positive feedback into those kids.

Even now that many of them are in their 40s, she relentlessly praises and applauds them, still telling them to this day how special, talented, capable, and beautiful they are.

Yet now, as adults, they all suffer from severe low self-esteem. Each one of them lacks confidence. They even admit to thinking they are ugly.

How can this be? No one was ever loved and encouraged more than those six people. Their mother told them so often… why didn't they *listen*?

The answer is that kids, like most people, don't really listen.

They *watch*.

If you watched their mother, as I have, you'd noticed that every time she looks into a mirror she grimaces and comments on how ugly she is. Every time she sees a photograph of herself she winces and points out how unattractive she looks. When encouraged by a friend to try something new or to do something adventurous, she is quick to say that she could never do such a thing. "That's for other people," she says.

Those six kids didn't listen to what their mother said. They watched what she did and internalized how she felt about herself. When she looked in the mirror and winced, they thought, *If she thinks she's ugly and I look like her, I must be ugly too.*

When she refused to do something because she didn't believe she could, they thought, *If she couldn't do it—*this woman who was their idol, their rock, their mother—*then there's no way such a thing would be possible for me.*

When we were children, we quickly learned to tune out the voices of our parents and other authority figures. We did that quite consciously. It's how we started claiming our own identity. But unconsciously we never stopped watching.

This phenomenon is part of our evolution. Thousands of years ago, when we were still living in caves and carrying around cattle bones as clubs, a newborn needed to be accepted by the tribe or it was left behind to die. Over time, nature selected the ones who could mirror those around them to gain acceptance. We developed what neuroscientists call mirror neurons. You can see them in action when you take a picture of someone smiling and you find yourself automatically smiling, too. Your mirror neurons did that. These mirror neurons are always working below the level of your consciousness. It's why people will eventually model and match your behavior, particularly the behavior of the one deemed "leader."

I see this mirroring phenomenon played out in many of the large organizations I speak to. If the leaders of one company dress professionally and wear custom-made suits, lo and behold, the entire auditorium of their people are dressed to the nines in suits. Another organization's leaders in the same industry might wear ripped designer jeans, T-shirts, and dog tags, and guess what? The whole audience looks like their clones.

I'd bet most of the people in those organizations didn't dress like that before they joined, but over time they started unconsciously emulating, adapting to, and mirroring their leaders. Your teams will do the same.

YOU'RE ALWAYS ON STAGE

So what's the overarching lesson here? Who you are, how you show up, how you act, live, and represent yourself is your greatest source of influence, and your people will, without even knowing it, mirror your lead.

"Your people don't listen to you, but they do watch you. They are always watching. BE the example."

@DarrenHardy #JoinTheRide

You are on stage at all times.

Every room you enter, every conversation you engage in, everywhere you are, you are being watched by those around you. Think about the interactions you've had in the past few days. Did you show up promptly, enthusiastically, and joyfully? Were you an example of your best self? Were people uplifted by your presence, conversation, observations, and encouragement? Or were you complaining, joining the gossip, and perpetuating the defeatist dialogue? Whatever your example, rest assured, you got matching results, even if you didn't notice.

Every action, comment, and reaction you put out there is training your team. They're simply reflecting what you project, and if you want to change the reflection, you have to change the projection. You have to lead by example.

2. LEADERS DO WHAT'S UNPOPULAR

"It must be nice to be in charge."

How many times have you heard that statement? How many times have you *said* that statement, or wished *you* were in charge?

Now you are.

Once you really are the leader, though, you quickly discover that leadership *isn't* always that "nice." It's not easy or fun. It's hard work. And not just hard in the long, demanding hours sense (though the hours *are* long and demanding), but *emotionally* hard.

In July 2008, Starbucks CEO Howard Schultz agonized over the decision to lay off thousands of employees and close 600 stores, 70 percent of which had only been built and opened in the past few years. He calls it the most painful day in his professional life. "The decision to close that many stores was tough," he said. "But it wasn't stores, it was people."

He recalled the moment he made the announcement to his headquarters team: "It was a very emotional moment for me where I couldn't hold myself together. I was looking at people whom I'd known for ten to fifteen years who I was now asking to leave. It was a heartbreak."

While he knew it would make him very unpopular to thousands of people, particularly to those people whose lives would immediately change based on his decision, he also knew it was the right decision and one he had to make to save the company and its future.

He said, "I was faced with the burden and responsibility of saving the company. In order to preserve and ultimately enhance the company, I had to make emotional and highly charged (unpopular) decisions that in the short term were really going to fracture the lives of people."

ENTREPRENEUR

Like Schultz, you're going to have to make tough calls, too.

You might have to make the tough decision to abandon a big marketing and distribution channel like Michael Dell did when he decided to pull out of Walmart (and all retail) to focus his company on its direct-to-consumer model. It was a decision that revolutionized the computer sales industry back in 1993.

You might have to shut down existing profit centers like former CEO of McDonald's Jim Skinner did when he sold off controlling interest in the Chipotle brand and all other non-McDonald's businesses in 2006 in order to "remove distractions" and "get back to basics." Profit more than doubled under Skinner's reign as leader.

You might need to step in and terminate entire product lines as Steve Jobs did when he returned to lead a nearly bankrupt Apple in 1997. Those, and other difficult decisions, propelled the company to ultimately being deemed the world's most valuable brand.

Rest assured, if your name badge is going to say "leader," you will be called to ruffle feathers, ride roughshod over poor performance, fire nice people, kill sacred cows, terminate pet projects, and veto the democratic vote.

All of which will likely make you very unpopular.

But the aim of the leader is not to be liked. It's to *lead*. To do the right thing. And more often than we like, the right thing is not the popular thing.

"When people are calling you out and calling you names, they're really just calling you a leader."

@DarrenHardy #JoinTheRide

Are you willing to make the difficult choices? To do what's unpopular? It's not easy, but remember this: When people are calling you out and calling you names, they're really just calling you a *leader*.

3. LEADERS GROW OTHERS

I went to school with a shy, quiet girl named Cassie.

Through her entire childhood, Cassie had been told, "If you don't have something important to say, Cassie, don't say anything at all." Throughout most of her childhood, she heard, "That's not important, Cassie," "Nobody cares, Cassie," "Be quiet, Cassie." By the time I got to know her a little bit in high school, most people referred to her as "the girl who never speaks."

In my junior year of high school, we had Mr. Wilson for A.P. English. Mr. Wilson was a different kind of teacher. He didn't lecture much, but he asked a lot of questions of students. And instead of lining the desks up in rows like the other teachers did, he organized them in a circle, always including a desk for himself.

One day we were discussing *Romeo and Juliet.* Though this was about the pre-Leonardo DiCaprio and Claire Danes version, the class was still animated—there's just something about that rebellious teenage love story that gets teenagers all fired up. Students were throwing their opinions at each other like a wild game of dodgeball. Mr. Wilson delighted in our enthusiasm and acted as our referee, strategically posing questions to keep the discussion moving forward from student to student.

At one point, during a particularly heated discussion about the death scene, Mr. Wilson noticed something the rest of us missed: Cassie had taken a small breath, the kind you take when you have something you want to say.

Mr. Wilson stopped the other students mid-sentence. He turned to her. "Cassie," he said, gently, "is there something you would like to add?"

Wide-eyed, the entire class turned to her and waited. Would she speak? Cassie shifted forward (No way! She's going to say something!), then shrank back into her seat. (Nope, she's not.)

Mr. Wilson asked again. "Cassie, I can see you have something to add, and I would be delighted to hear it—we all would." He motioned to the class, nodding, and we nodded in return. Cassie raised her eyes toward Mr. Wilson. They were bright blue, innocent, and scared. And after a long pause she whispered, "It's not important," as her voice trailed off and she looked back to the ground, as if hoping to disappear into it.

"Leave her alone, Mr. Wilson," one student said.

"Yeah, Mr. Wilson, Cassie doesn't like to speak in class."

Mr. Wilson quieted everyone. We watched as he rose to his feet, walked across the middle of the circle, and crouched down in front of Cassie's desk.

"Cassie, you are a smart, witty, and extremely wise young woman. I have had the honor of reading your essays all semester, and I know we would *all* find great value in any insights you want to share. Believe me when I say that anything you have to share is important. Always."

Slowly, Cassie lifted her gaze. She looked around at a room full of 17-year-old faces, captivated by this interaction, and murmuring in agreement that yes, they *did* want to hear what she had to say—that it *was* important.

That morning, for the first time since we had known her, Cassie spoke in class.

I don't remember exactly what she said—something about the knife and Juliet breaking patterns of female archetypes—but whatever it was, it sounded pretty good to me. What I *do* remember clearly was the real-life metamorphosis that happened before my eyes. This once inconspicuous caterpillar transformed into a butterfly. For the rest of the semester, she sat tall and beamed as she spoke. From then on, every rapid-fire discussion that took place had Cassie right in the middle of it.

Mr. Wilson taught me a lot that day about what it means to truly *be* a leader. He taught me that leaders don't tell you what to think, they encourage you to think for yourself. They don't dictate, they facilitate— they arrange chairs in circles and sit alongside you. He taught me that people and ideas thrive in the process of engagement and co-creation.

Perhaps the greatest lesson Mr. Wilson taught me that day is that many times the greatest contributor is not the loudest or the most confident. He showed me that as a leader, you must look for those small intakes of breath from the quieter members of your team. And when you hear one, gently and persistently encourage that person to speak. Every voice is important.

It is the responsibility of the leader to draw out the talent, drive, and capability of the people on their team. Most people are operating at a fraction of what they are really capable of. As the leader, you will need to find the unique seeds of greatness buried in each member of your team. You need to remove the weeds (fears, inhibitions, uncertainties), water and fertilize (invest in their personal growth), and provide the sunshine (your positive attitude, belief in them, and example) to transform that miraculous seed inside them into a bountiful harvest of results and productivity.

> ## "The leader's responsibility is to draw out the talent, drive, and capability of the people on your team. Your job as a leader is to grow your people."
>
> @DarrenHardy #JoinTheRide

167

It's easy to be distracted by the job of growing your business. But never forget that your job as a leader is also to grow *people*.

4. LEADERS LET OTHERS LEAD

A few years ago, I had the chance to ask a billionaire how he achieved the proverbial "B" status. His answer—which was only three words long—floored me. Ever since then, I have been trying to master his advice.

At the time, his net worth was about three billion dollars. That makes his answer worth about a billion dollars per *word*.

Here's what he told me:

"Be a quitter."

Did you just say, "Huh"?

Yeah, that's what I said, too.

But he wasn't being trite. "Be a quitter" truly was his advice, and he felt that it was the secret to his Big B status.

"Whatever you are doing in your business right now," he told me, "your goal really is to find a way to quit it. You need to stop doing almost everything you do at the office."

He could see I was perplexed (as I'm sure you are now too), so he explained further.

"Once the founder has the vision, the key to achieving that vision is to delegate—as much and as fast as possible. Delegation is a form of quitting. Even if you are the most well-rounded and capable CEO of all time, you are still better off delegating functions to specialists. This allows you to multiply the size of your endeavor through large numbers of people rather than trying to do everything yourself.

"The process of quitting is really trying to give up every part of your job as fast as you can," he said. "All the parts that is, *except* the part of being the visionary leader."

"*Easier said than done...*" I mumbled under my breath. The billionaire chuckled.

"Look, when you first start a business, you're likely going to have to do everything—sales, customer service, accounting, all the way down to taking out the trash. Your goal is to get enough sales going so you can quit taking out the trash and hire someone else to do it. Get more sales going, then quit doing the accounting. Hire a specialist to do it. Get more sales going and quit doing customer service, too. You want to go from everything to nothing—except leading. You only get there by quitting everything as fast as you can."

He concluded by saying, "You want to turn labor into leadership. As the founder and CEO, you should not be doing anything. You should only be leading."

This is brilliant advice.

"You can't be a great leader if you spend your time doing tasks that aren't actually leadership."

@DarrenHardy #JoinTheRide

The reason most people don't make it to billionaire status is because they're doing the opposite. They are taking on more and more tasks for which they are not the most skilled or best suited. When you are not a specialist at something, results are diminished. And when you're doing more and more tasks, you're simultaneously diminishing your ability to do what your *real* specialty needs to become: *lead*.

You can't lead if you're designing brochures.

You can't lead if you're doing accounting.

You can't lead if you're managing production.

You can't be a great leader if you keep doing things that aren't actually leadership.

Get out of the way. Let others take the lead on those roles. You're the head coach, not the player. Imagine if the head coach ran onto the field to throw a pass, make a block, or intercept a throw. They'd throw him out of the stadium. But business leaders are doing that to their people all the time.

Be a quitter. Do your *real* job, and let your team do theirs.

KNOW WHEN TO LET GO

Twenty years ago I started a professional training and development company with a partner. We started it organically (a fancy way of saying "we had nothing"—no money, no people, nothing). We needed help in the office but didn't have the revenue to pay someone.

There we were, stuck right smack between a rock and a hard place, when an idea came to us: Diana!

Diana had worked for my partner in a previous venture. She was capable and, as luck would have it, available. Fortunately for us, she was also open-minded.

We called Diana in for an official meeting in my partner's living-room-turned-office and pitched her on our big vision. We promised her that if she would be willing to work for free—for just a little while—that's all we'd need! Soon we'd be rolling in money and able to compensate her generously. She bought our story, hopped on board our dream-ship, and started working for us pro bono.

When it came to her job description, she didn't really have one—Diana did a little bit of everything. She handled the bookkeeping, set up our event logistics, booked our travel, tracked our marketing results—whatever came up, Diana tried to figure it out.

It didn't take long for our business to become the big success we had promised, and when I handed Diana her first paycheck, I don't know whose smile was bigger, hers or mine!

However, while we were right about the fact that our company would grow, we seriously underestimated how quickly it would happen. Before we knew it, we had outgrown Diana's skill set. We needed an experienced CFO. We needed a professional event manager. We needed a veteran marketing director.

At first, we weren't too concerned—certainly there was a place for Diana. But when we tried her in several different positions, nothing worked. Either she didn't like the role, or she wasn't equipped for it. Determined, we sent Diana to several training classes to develop her skills in other areas, but still, it just wasn't enough for what we needed.

We loved Diana. But we were jeopardizing the business to keep her.

I hate to let people go. I can't sleep the entire night before. I remember it was a Friday afternoon when we finally decided to say goodbye to Diana. I called her into my office, and as she walked in, all the color drained from my face. *There's got to be another way*, I thought, *maybe she could...*

I desperately tried to conjure up a last-minute position that would suit both Diana and the company's needs, but we were out of options. It was time for Diana to go. I could barely speak the words I needed to say, and when I did, she started to cry. And I started to cry.

I handed her a check for a six-month severance and helped her pack her things.

It was finally done.

Sometimes, there comes a point, even after all of the growing, after all of the caring, after all of the dreaming and delegating, when there is really nothing else that can be done except to let someone go. It's part of the leader's job, and employees across the world are getting fired every minute. But that doesn't make it any easier on the leader who has to do it.

When the day comes that you're facing this crossroad, I want you to consider this quote from Reed Hastings, the CEO of Netflix. He points out a subtle but profound distinction—one that has helped me in these difficult moments.

In a discussion with his own team, he said:

171

"We are a team, not a family. It is the coach's job at every level to hire, develop, and cut smartly so we have stars in every position."

—Reed Hastings #JoinTheRide

"We are a team, not a family. We're like a pro sports team, not a recreational kids' team. It is the coach's job at every level of Netflix to hire, develop, and cut smartly so we have stars in every position."

Why a "team" and not a "family"? A family culture sets up a mindset of entitlement and privilege. After all, you can't fire your brother-in-law or get on the case of your mother for not pulling her weight.

A pro sports team culture elicits an entirely different attitude. You are either performing at the level the team needs, or you get cut or traded. Nothing personal. If it's going to win, the team needs to be able to rely on the best person in every position. And the coach's job (you) is to recruit, develop, and trade up for the best player in every one of those positions. Every chair in the office needs to be the best it can be.

There is one last twist to the Diana story. A few months later, I was at a friend's intimate vineyard wedding in the Napa Valley. During the cocktail hour, while the guests were mingling, I approached the bar and who did I see… but Diana. She was working with the owners of the vineyard, learning the elegant details of the wine business, and managing the guest experiences.

I'll admit, it was a little awkward at first—for both of us. But after the initial shock, she poured me a glass of her favorite cabernet and admitted that the last few months working for us hadn't been great. She was overwhelmed, stressed, and unhappy. "I would have stayed forever," she said. "And I would have been miserable." Now she was living her dream life and thanked us for having the courage to let her go.

We raised a glass to her happiness, and as I walked to join my friends at dinner (drinking my new favorite wine), I felt happy, too.

THE GIFT OF LEADERSHIP

Every entrepreneur who leads also feels the weight of responsibility for those who follow. Day after day, you are significantly influencing people's lives—often in ways you don't even realize. People will look to you. They'll emulate you. Your ride will provide them with challenges, opportunities to grow, a livelihood, and the chance to do something that matters.

It's an awesome responsibility. Take it seriously.

With that responsibility, though, comes a grand opportunity—one that brings with it the highest rewards. I'm not talking about success and bank deposits (although those are great, too!). I'm talking about the fulfillment you get from knowing you have left the indelible imprint of making a truly positive difference in someone's life. It's a profoundly rewarding experience and a great privilege—one you should accept with honor and dignity.

"Everyone in your organization is learning how to think, act, and react from YOU. Lead by example."

@DarrenHardy #JoinTheRide

Those sitting in the roller coaster cars behind you are watching you. They're taking their cues—at work and at home—from you. They're learning how to think, act, and react based on *what you do*.

How you ride? That's how *they* ride.

You're in the front seat now. So put a big smile on your face, shoot your arms up into the air, and shout, "Look! No hands!"

ACTION PLAN

GO TO THE RESOURCE PAGE AND COMPLETE THE WORKSHEETS ON:

■ Assessing your current leadership: What to evaluate and how to rate yourself and how to double-check

■ Building leaders: The 12 most important attributes you want to build and the plan for doing so

Go to: RollerCoasterBook.com/Resources

**Productivity is never an accident.
It is always the result of a commitment to excellence, intelligent planning, and focused effort.**
—Paul J. Meyer

CHAPTER 6
PICKING UP SPEED

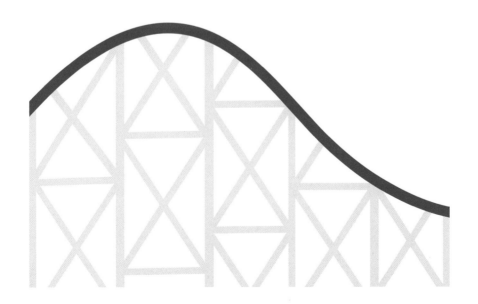

BECOME INSANELY PRODUCTIVE WITHOUT LOSING YOUR MIND

To say I am a hardworking guy would be an understatement. The son of an achievement-driven college football coach, I was trained, drilled, and intimidated into working hard and grinding it out. Whatever it took, buckle down, no whining, no crying, no excuses. By the time I was a teenager, I started to realize this was quite an advantage. I was certainly never the smartest or most talented in anything I competed for—grades, sports, or sales. But I could out-hustle and out-work anyone. I wore it like a badge of honor. Applying relentless brute force, I could achieve most any goal I set.

By the time I was thirty-five, I had accomplished quite a bit, but I was killing myself. All I was doing was working. Brute force became brutal. I was sacrificing nights, weekends, friendships, vacations, and, well, most everything.

But then I interviewed a few of the greats—I sat down with guys like Richard Branson, Tony Hawk, and Steve Wynn—and even though I was working my *tail* off, by almost any measure of success I used, all three of these guys were kicking my butt! They are wealthier than I am. They're making a greater impact on the world than I do. *And* they have more joy, more freedom, and are taking the time to enjoy the fruits of their labor much more often than I am. When I realized this firsthand, I have to admit, it really ticked me off!

There is no doubt that I definitely spend a lot less time frolicking on the beach than Branson does on his private island. I know for a fact I spend less time than Wynn does on the golf course. And unquestionably

I spend a lot less time with my personal hobbies, my family, and my friends than Tony Hawk does.

Worst of all? I spend a lot *more* time working than they do!

Here is the epiphany I came to: If busyness, long hours, and hard work equaled success, I'd be wealthier and more successful than Richard Branson, Tony Hawk, and Steve Wynn. But I'm not… because busyness, long hours, and hard word *do not* necessarily equal success.

"That's it," I thought after shaking their hands after their interviews. "I *have* to figure this out."

How were they doing it? We all started in roughly the same place, with the same 24-hour day and the same opportunities. Yet I'm getting my butt kicked? While doing *more*? There's gotta be something I'm doing wrong.

And there was.

And I bet you're doing it wrong, too.

YOUR SUCCESS VITALS

Let's say, heaven forbid, you are in a serious accident and are rushed to the hospital. What's the first thing that happens? Before they address the gash on your face, before they even think about the bone sticking out of your thigh, even before they contact your loved ones, where do the skilled physicians in the emergency room begin?

They start with your vital signs.

They don't concern themselves with extremities or facial deformities; they start with your vitals—your heart rate, respiratory rate, blood pressure, and body temperature. Why? Because your vitals are just that—vital! These are the key *life or death* physiological indicators. What is the point of sewing up your leg if your dropping blood pressure is causing the leg tissue to die even as it's being repaired? Sure, the drama of a protruding bone might be distracting to an untrained eye, but medical personnel know that the discipline of assessing vital signs tells a great deal without asking a single question or performing a single invasive test. It saves precious moments when moments are all you have.

This is also true about your business and your personal productivity. There are vital factors that determine the life or death of your business and performance. It's easy to get caught up in the drama of extremities, to respond to symptoms all day and end up with a dead business—without even knowing why.

The reason is you lost sight of the vital factors—those few things that mattered the most but weren't necessarily the loudest, most urgent, or most obvious. But they were the most important.

I have found that most people who read a magazine like *SUCCESS* or would read a book like this (especially this far—bravo!) don't need motivation. They don't lack ambition, goals, or work ethic. They are putting in long hours, sacrificing nights and weekends, and consistently have their nose to the grindstone. Like me, they'll use brute force and sacrifice whatever they have to… all the while lacking clarity and focus. They are unsure of what to focus on, so they attempt to focus on everything all the time. Thus they end up overworked, overscheduled, overwhelmed, and still underperforming… maybe even failing

It's not that they didn't work; it's what they worked on that caused the failure.

I know you have big goals and an important mission to accomplish. To succeed, it is critical that you intensely focus your time, energy, and resources on those things that matter most—your vital factors—without being distracted and derailed by the things that matter least.

In this chapter, I am going to outline the four vital factors critical to managing and leading yourself, your team, and your business. If you can be unrelenting in your focus, accountability, and constant improvement of these four vital factors, you will have your hands on the controls that will allow you to transform one of the most frustrating emotional drops on your roller coaster ride into one of the greatest, most thrilling highs, as your ride becomes a rocket ship that can carry you "to infinity and beyond."

1. YOUR VITAL FUNCTIONS

I got a diagnosis of my productivity problem from a doctor, no less.

Not just any doctor—"America's Doctor." Several years ago I interviewed Dr. Mehmet Oz for his (first) cover profile in *SUCCESS*.

This man *is* a wizard. Great and powerful.

I am in awe of everything this amazing man gets accomplished. He is a professor at Columbia University and directs the Cardiovascular Institute at New York Presbyterian Hospital. He's authored 400 research papers, several medical books, and six *New York Times* best-selling books. He runs a thriving nonprofit, is co-founder of another successful company, has a four-time Emmy Award–winning TV show... and at the time of our interview, he was still performing over 200 open heart surgeries a year.

What's most amazing is that he does it all with grace, poise, and tranquility. When I was with him, he was relaxed, gracious, and adoringly humble. And before you ask, let me tell you: He's also a devoted husband and father of four. Now you'd *have* to be a wizard to pull all that off, right? Well, he does have one secret.

181

Here is the secret I was given by the great wizard called Oz. When I asked the question, "How on *earth*...?" He said, "I've figured out that every endeavor that you do has a few vital functions. All you have to do is figure out what they are and become excellent at them."

He gave the example of open heart surgery. He explained he isn't involved with *all* the functions of a successful procedure, just the few *vital* ones. He isn't the one to clean the instruments or make up the operating table or get the supplies ready. He doesn't even do the several dozen procedures happening inside the body cavity that lead up to his vital few. When it comes time for those vital few, he walks in and performs them with excellence and well-developed expertise, removes his mask, washes his hands, and exits, leaving the rest of the procedure to his capable team.

The exact same is true for delivering his high-quality TV show. There are a few vital functions he needs to prepare for, practice, and be ready to deliver with excellence. Everything else is handled by the great team he surrounds himself with. It's the same for writing his books, the same for running a charity, and the same when it comes to leading a business.

There it is. What's the big secret of how to get it all done? Don't. Just do the vital functions (amazingly well) and build a great team of capable players who are excellent at the rest (which you already learned how to do in Chapter 4).

> # "The big secret of how to get it all done? Don't. Just do the vital functions (amazingly well) and build a great team who are excellent at the rest."
>
> @DarrenHardy #JoinTheRide

What I realized after our interview was this was the same idea I had applied to my real estate business two decades earlier. I had just forgotten to keep applying it when I changed my business focus.

Starting out in real estate, I had quickly discovered there were thousands of things I could get caught up doing—things that *felt* productive, but were really just a convenient distraction from doing real work (aka prospecting and making sales). Things like setting up escrow files, taking photos of the property, ordering the property report, setting up the termite inspection, meeting with the appraiser, going to the home inspection, putting on the lockbox, and attending the escrow closing can keep even the hardest-working agent *very* busy. They all seem like legitimate tasks that should be done, and in fact, yes, they *should* be done. Just not by the rainmaker!

The rainmaker has one job—make it rain!

I soon realized there were only a few things that I did that mattered. As the leader, when I did them, we got paid. I couldn't delegate them.

They were my vital functions in the business. They were:

1. **Pitching a listing,**
2. **Negotiating a contract**
3. **Prospecting.**

That's it. Those three things. Those were my vital few functions. They were critical to business growth, and I needed to be (and was) great at them. They were the only things I should spend my time on, so I built a team that did all those other things. When I started spending most of my time doing those vital few functions, the business took off like a rocket!

Though… I'd be lying if I said it didn't take some practice.

TIME "ON"

In my real estate business, when I got clear about this idea of doing *only the vital few functions*, I decided I really needed to drive the message home to myself and to my team. So I bought a stopwatch and wore it around my neck all day. I turned it on every time I did one of those vital three functions and turned it off the split second I stopped.

I'll never forget the first day I put that stopwatch to the test. I wanted to set the bar really, really high. I wanted to put in a ton of vital time so I would have to struggle to match that goal every day thereafter. I arrived at the office with my mind set on doing nothing but vital functions for the next 16 hours.

Immediately, I hit the streets for some door-to-door prospecting. I'd walk up a driveway, knock on the door, and when it opened, I'd hit the watch. When I was done talking, I'd stop it. Repeat. Then I moved to cold calls and did the same thing. If I was pitching a listing? Same thing. Start the watch, stop the watch. Negotiating? Same thing. All the while I wouldn't look at the stopwatch—I didn't want to see the number until the day was complete.

At ten o'clock that night I finally stopped cranking and the suspense was killing me! I closed the final file on my tidied desk, let out a sigh, and for the first time since before the sun had risen that morning, I turned the clock over expecting to see at *least* 14 hours of vital work logged on the screen…

Can you guess what that (evil) stopwatch said?

Not 14 hours, that's for sure.

19:54

Less than 20 minutes out of a 16-hour day.

If you had asked anyone in my office if I was productive all 16 hours, they'd have said, "Oh yeah, he's a machine." And I was indeed a constant flurry of activity.

But activity is not productivity.

After my abysmal failure that first day, I became obsessed. Every day it was me against the stopwatch as I tried to drive that number up. Doubling it to forty minutes was a herculean effort. The first time I got it over an hour I threw an office-wide party to celebrate. I think in the four-year career I had in real estate sales, I got the number over four hours maybe a dozen times. Which means what? Yeah, a dozen times in four years, I worked a *half-day*.

I challenge you to take on the stopwatch. Once you identify what your vital functions *are,* start tracking how much time you actually spend *doing* them. You will be shocked at how little time you're spending on the most important things, the *only* things, you should be spending your time on. If you make it your mission to increase that number, you'll change your business and your life.

"Success has less to do with what we can get ourselves to do and more with keeping ourselves from doing what we shouldn't."

@DarrenHardy #JoinTheRide

UNDERSTANDING YOUR VALUE

In our July 2010 *SUCCESS* feature with Kenneth Cole, he said it this way: "Success has less to do with what we can get ourselves to do and more to do with keeping ourselves from doing what we shouldn't."

Make sense? Sure. But *how?* If the greatest threat to your productivity is keeping yourself from getting awash in low-value activities, how do you make sure you don't mistake a low-value activity for a high one? Here's how I do it:

First, you need to know what your time is worth. And I'm not talking in some warm and fuzzy Kumbaya terms. I'm talking cold, hard cash. What does your time need to be worth in order to accomplish the goals you've set for yourself?

What's your income goal for the year? $100,000? $500,000? $1,000,000? Divide that number by 2,000.

The number you get is the hourly rate you have to generate over a 40-hour week in the next year.

Every hour that goes by that you don't produce that amount, you're falling behind. Got it? No? Then try this instead:

For a goal of $250,000 a year, your hourly rate must be $125. So let's say on January 1 of the new year, you wake up with $250,000 deposited into your bank account (Happy New Year indeed!). Now every hour you do less than *$125 per hour work*, $125 gets taken out of your account (remember this accounting system is based on doing valuable work, not just busywork). Now let's say it's December 31 and you look in your account and see there is only $64,375 remaining! You say, "What happened? I worked long, exhaustive hours all year. More than 2,000 hours! I sacrificed nights and weekends. I wrote my $250,000 goal down every morning. What went wrong?" It's simple… do the math. Every hour you did less than $125-per-hour-caliber work, you lost money.

If you're falling short of your income goals, it's because you waste time doing low-value work. That's it. That's the only reason. You go to a meeting you don't actually need to attend. You spend ten minutes chit-chatting in the hallway. You take an extra long lunch because you *deserve* it.

Do you? Do you deserve it? No. You deserve more than this.

When you spend twenty minutes on social media, you are burning time. Burning $100 bills.

Stop doing that. Now.

All you have in life is time. Your job is to maximize it, particularly when it's "ON" time.

No More Narcissism

You're probably asking, "Okay, how do I stick to my three vital functions when all these other things still have to get done?"

The answer is simple. You need to delegate everything anyone else can do at a lower rate to free up every minute possible for you to do your vital functions. You need to be constantly asking yourself, "Would I pay someone (the hourly rate you just determined above) to do what I'm doing now?" Ask yourself that when you are commenting on Facebook or organizing your files or driving across town to drop off papers or organizing the icons on your computer screen. If your answer is "no," then *stop* doing it yourself. It's costing you money. You can't afford to do it. You have to delegate.

It's funny (and kind of sad) because most CEOs will stand in front of their staff meeting, and in an effort to provide hope and inspiration, they'll say, "I once started out in the mailroom of this company, and now I'm CEO." But as soon as the meeting is over, they spend the next 45 minutes sorting through their inboxes, processing and responding to their own email...

"Your inbox is nothing more than a modern-day mailroom. Is that really where you want to be working?"

@DarrenHardy #JoinTheRide

Do you know what an inbox actually is?

The modern-day *mailroom!*

Congrats, CEO—you have come all that way just to end up back where you started.

You already know you need to delegate more, but you don't. Why? Because you are an egotistical, arrogant narcissist! It's true. At least that is what a mentor once told me when I made excuses to him about why it's just easier, faster, and better for me to do it than to ask someone else to do it.

With patience and a little irritation in his voice, my mentor said, "Darren, delegation requires humility. A recognition that you aren't the only one who can do something well, quickly, and competently. Stop being a narcissist and let go."

Whoa, that got my attention. Lo and behold, he was right. I found that not only did others get it done as well, but in almost every case they did the work *better* than I would have. My "letting go" meant they could step up and exercise strengths and abilities I didn't even know they had. They were allowed to focus on their expertise while I focused on mine. Together we could multiply the productive output of the entire organization.

Now let's go even deeper…

THE ONE THING

Several years ago now, when I sat with Joel Osteen and his wife in their home in Houston, Texas, I was determined to learn one thing from this man of many talents. The only questions I planned to ask were: "How do you do it all? How do you oversee, manage, and lead this massive enterprise?" His answer revolutionized the way I work—and for those with whom I have shared it, the same is true. Joel's response detailed a journey all entrepreneurs must take.

"When I first took over from my father, I was trying to do everything," Joel said. "Weddings, funerals, baptisms, I was trying to do it all. I was editing the brochure, the TV commercials. I was adjusting the lights on the stage. And the organization became stagnant. It could only grow as much as my calendar could stretch. I was burned out, and the organization was stalled. Something had to change.

"So I stepped back and I thought, what is the one thing I do that makes the biggest difference to the whole enterprise? And I figured out it was the 22 minutes on Sunday—that broadcast that then gets shot around the world. If it's great, it propels everything else. So I stopped doing everything else and began to focus only on those 22 minutes."

Wow. Wonder what that kind of focus looks like? Here's Joel's actual schedule. (Go ahead, copy it down and tape it to your bathroom mirror—this is good stuff!)

Wednesday he spends the whole day thinking and researching and making notes about what he wants to talk about Sunday.

Thursday he writes out his sermon word for word.

Friday he spends the *entire* day just memorizing it. That's all.

Saturday he delivers the sermon twice to a private audience in his church.

Sunday? Lights, camera, action, and BAM, he's magic. It's magic because he focused all his energy all week in making it so.

Monday he takes off. R&R.

Tuesday he does leadership. He goes in to the office, does his leadership oversight, and inspects what he expects. Those are also the days he does any media. I've interviewed him twice, and guess what day it was on? Yep. Tuesday.

Osteen has taken the "three vital functions" a step further. He's figured out his *one vital function.*

What's yours? What's your one thing that contributes the most to your enterprise?

What is your greatest contribution to making your rocket ship fly?

Figure that out, and then plot, scheme, and strategize about how to spend more, if not all, your time doing that one thing.

Do that, and *life will change for you.*

2. YOUR VITAL PRIORITIES

If you've ever been to an old-style circus or seen one on TV, then you're almost certainly familiar with the classic image of the lion tamer—a dashing man in a red tuxedo and top hat who steps into a cage with the king of the jungle himself.

The lion dwarfs the lion tamer. He's faster and more aggressive. He's 500 pounds of evolutionarily honed killing machine. He's a predator at the top of the food chain with rippling muscles and razor-sharp fangs and claws.

And the lion tamer?

He's got a stool.

That's it. Just a piece of flimsy *furniture*.

Yet, using nothing but that stool, the tamer is able to not only protect himself from the lion but also actually *control* the lion.

How is it possible that a lion tamer—a tiny man in a silly suit—can control a lion using nothing more than a barstool and a measly whip?

The answer is that the lion sees each of the legs of the barstool as four separate, simultaneous threats. In the face of those four threats, even the king of the jungle is overwhelmed. His primitive brain is unable to cope or decide, so he simply submits to the overwhelming threat. He becomes docile.

We respond similarly. We, too, suffer from the "lion syndrome." As an entrepreneur, you're faced with hundreds of potential priorities in any moment. Do you follow up on a sales call? Check email? Contact a vendor? Deal with the new hire? Work on a new product that's behind schedule? There are so many choices in each moment, and each one feels important. *Everything* seems important. But when you have too many priorities, like the lion, you become paralyzed—docile, and easily subdued by... well, furniture. (Ever notice how comfortable the couch feels when you're overwhelmed?)

Choosing and narrowing your priorities mean *everything* on the entrepreneur roller coaster.

If you find yourself paralyzed at work, it means you have too many priorities. If you think you don't have enough time, it means you don't

189

ENTREPRENEUR

have priorities that are defined clearly enough. In fact, anytime you feel overwhelmed, there's a good chance that the culprit is a lack of clear priorities.

"Anytime you feel overwhelmed, there's a good chance the culprit is a lack of clear priorities."

@DarrenHardy #JoinTheRide

Let me make the clear distinction between a Vital Function and a Vital Priority. Vital Functions are your key contributions to the success of the organization or goal. Vital Priorities are the day-to-day or quarter-to-quarter areas of focus and tasks required to accomplish the goal.

For instance, my three Vital Functions at *SUCCESS* are keynote speaking to large audiences; creating, editing, and curating content; and public media representation. Whereas my Vital Priorities for the week might include preparing a keynote, final sign-off on an issue of *SUCCESS* going to press, and preparing for a TV appearance. Vital Functions are those few "rainmaking" roles you have and Vital Priorities are the important tasks you are focused on to fulfill those functions.

IT'S TIME TO DECLINE

I witnessed one of the great achievers of our time using this *exact* principle. If you're wondering how to translate the principles of lion taming to your business, here's a great example.

After our cover feature on Sir Richard Branson, a client company asked us to contact Sir Richard on their behalf to request hiring him to speak at their conference. They had a budget of $100,000 for a one-hour keynote. As a favor, we had someone from our staff inquire. Sir Richard's office flatly declined the offer. Undeterred, the company upped their offer to $250,000 for a one-hour talk. Again we reached out, but Sir Richard quickly declined.

They once again raised the speaking fee, now to $500,000, including a private jet to pick Sir Richard up. Sir Richard declined. At this point, it was becoming kind of an ego issue, so our client went all in and offered a blank check. "Let him name his number," they said. Once more we reached out on their behalf. "The client will pay whatever it takes," we said. "How much would it cost for Sir Richard to attend?"

Here's the response from his office:

"No amount of money would matter. Right now, Richard has three strategic priorities he is focused on, and he will only allow us to allocate his calendar to something that significantly contributes to the accomplishment of one of those three priorities, and speaking for a fee is not one of them."

There it is.

Priorities clear, protected, and steadfast.

No one is taming the lion that is Sir Richard Branson.

Not for any fee.

THE BUFFETT METHOD OF PRIORITIZATION

Perhaps the greatest "mystery" of the many achievers we feature in *SUCCESS* is how they manage to do it all. From the outside, they seem almost superhuman, accomplishing in a year what some of us only dream of in a lifetime.

> # "How do the superachievers do it all? The secret is they DON'T. What's your ONE priority?"
> @DarrenHardy #JoinTheRide

The answer to how they do it all, of course, is that *they don't.*

Branson's strict focus on where to spend his time is a perfect example of a recurring theme in superachievers: having *three* (or fewer) strategic priorities.

Here is Warren Buffett's three-step method for prioritization.

1. Write down all your priorities.
2. Narrow it down to the top three.

So far so good, right? Seems simple. No problem. You've done that before. It's the next step where most people don't have the courage to do what it takes to stay focused. And it's this final step that separates the simple achievers from the superachievers.

3. *Throw the rest of the list away.*

There's no *minor project list*. There's no *maybe we'll get to this list*. There's no *side project list*. There are only three priorities, and everything else is thrown out so all mental, financial, and spiritual resources can be fully invested into those three, and only those three, priorities.

"If you have more than three priorities, you don't have any."

@DarrenHardy #JoinTheRide

As Jim Collins said in our April 2010 *SUCCESS* feature, "If you have more than three priorities, you don't have any." How many do you have? Do you have the *chutzpah* to use the Buffett method?

THE MASTER SKILL OF SUCCESS

I can sense your doubt. I can hear you mumbling under your breath— as if throwing the rest of the list away is not a luxury you have. Of course, throwing the list away doesn't mean the distractions and attention-stealing interruptions go away, too, but that's because you still have to learn the single success skill that all superachievers have mastered…

Saying "no."

The only way for the attention-stealing interruptions to go away is for them not to be there in the first place! The mastery skill that separates the common man from superachiever status is learning to say "no." For an entrepreneur, to whom every opportunity looks shiny and every idea sounds awesome, these two letters will become the most important in the entire alphabet.

When Warren Buffett was asked what he thought the single greatest key to his success was, I was expecting an economic theory lesson in high finance or insider tips on shrewd business negotiations from the "Oracle of Omaha." Instead this was his answer, "For every hundred great opportunities that are brought to me, I say 'no' ninety-nine times."

That's it. That's the $58.5 billion answer.

Warren Buffett's key to success is saying "no" ninety-nine times out of every hundred solicitations of his time or attention.

Buffett's not alone. When Steve Jobs was asked of all that he and Apple had created which he was most proud, his answer was, "I'm as proud of what we *don't* do as I am of what we do." All those amazing, breakthrough, change-the-way-we-experience-the-world-as-we-know-it products, and *that's* what he's proud of… the things they said "no" to.

Why? Why would anyone, especially Steve Jobs, be proud of that? Because saying "no" is hard. It's the master skill of success.

Steve went on to say, "People think focus means saying 'yes' to the thing you've got to focus on. But that's not what it means at all. It means saying 'no' to the hundred other good ideas that there are. You have to pick carefully. [Success] is saying 'no' to 1,000 things."

I've seen this same principle at work in every superachiever I've met. They all know how to say "no." You see, saying "yes" is easy.

Yes, I have a minute.
Yes, I'll take the call.
Yes, I'll take on that project.
Yes, I'll come out for happy hour.
Yes, I'll have another drink.
Yes, I'll have dessert, too.

There's no resistance in "yes." There's no struggle or conflict. No one's feelings are at stake when you say "yes." However saying "no" is much harder. That is why the master skill of superachievers is how they stay focused on what matters most. It's one of the great keys to their success—and yours. Learn the master skill. Master "no."

"What's the master skill of productivity? Learning to say 'no.'"

@DarrenHardy #JoinTheRide

Finally, one last word of warning. Every time you say "yes" to something, you're actually saying "no" to something else. Perhaps it's a bigger opportunity that now you have to turn down, or maybe it's simply precious time spent with your children. Whatever the stakes, make sure that the next time you consider saying "yes" (when you really should be saying "no"), it's a "Hell yeah!" or don't even consider it.

3. YOUR VITAL METRICS

Not long ago, I was catching up with a friend over dinner when the discussion turned to my work and in particular, my financial goals for the *SUCCESS* media business. I described in detail my plan for growing the multimillion-dollar business—how I'd get to one revenue point, and then the strategy I'd use to double that figure, and then double it again.

After a long period when I did all the talking and he just listened, there was a pause. And he asked (as only a real friend knows how to do), "Why?"

"Whaddya mean why?" I puffed back. "Because I can. Because I should. Because I want to."

"I know," he responded. "But *why*? Is it about the money?"

It wasn't about the money. It's never been about the money. Yes, when it comes to my business, I know all the victory metrics. But when it comes to the actual dollars and cents, my personal finances are handled almost entirely by my wife. For me, achieving *metrics* is achieving victory, not collecting money.

My friend then said something that rocked my world a bit. He said, "Then you are tracking the wrong metric."

I let that sink in before responding. I was tracking the wrong metric? It was true. I had just finished telling him about doubling revenue numbers when I really didn't care much about the revenue at all.

While I pondered, he continued, "Why do you do what you do?"

I was quick to respond, "Impact. To positively impact people's lives and futures." No need for contemplation there.

My friend replied, "Then measure that."

Huh. Whaddya know! He was right. For me it was about growing *impact,* not growing money. Once I realized that, it changed everything.

I looked at our customer base more closely, and I isolated a smaller group with whom I knew I had the biggest impact. I began to offer them opportunities to go *deeper.* Ways in which I could have a greater impact on their work, their health, their finances, and their relationships. Impact became the thing I measured to discover when I was on course and when I was off. It would tell me when I was getting closer to my goals—my *real* goals—and when I was moving further away.

Impact became my *vital metric.*

Measurement plays a key role on the entrepreneur roller coaster. First of all, it lets you know when you're off track. When was the last time you saw a roller coaster with a straight track? From beginning to end, there are unexpected twists and turns. Surprise dead-ends, reversals, and hairpin turns. Each time the track deviates, you need to readjust your course to head back toward your goal. Otherwise you could end up somewhere completely different from where you planned. But to do that, you need to know that you're *off* track to begin with.

Second, measurement helps you correct your course. When the ride takes you off course—and you *will* be taken off course—you'll need to know in which direction to head. Sometimes you'll have to go off course on *purpose* to avoid an obstacle, and measurement will bring you back.

Last, when you hit a low point in the ride and things seem darkest, measurement proves to you that you're making progress. Sure, you may not have arrived at your final destination, but you've covered a lot of ground. Imagine driving across the country and not knowing where you are. Ever. Measurement is your GPS and your odometer.

Just like a doctor measures your vital signs of health—things like your heart rate, blood pressure, and oxygen levels—you need to determine and keep a close eye on the vital metrics for you, your team, and your business. It is critical, as in life or death, that you know what these metrics are and that you keep a constant watchful eye on them—as in daily, if not hourly.

You should find about half a dozen metrics that summarize the critical data you need to monitor your business's progress and make effective decisions. You'll need to decide exactly what they are for your business, but they can be metrics like:

New sales transactions
Cancellations
Cash on hand total
Receivables total
Payables total

From there, I always break it down to the few measurements that drive the above metrics. For instance:

New database opt-ins
Face-to-face sales appointments
Store/website visits

There are always a few metrics that will ultimately make the ones you are pursuing downstream possible.

Then I take it one more step, much like Joel Osteen, and see if I can find just *one* economic denominator. The single most telling and determining metric that, if increased and improved, will be the factor contributing the most to all the other numbers being bolstered downstream. Now all I have to do is watch and plot, scheme, brainstorm, and focus on all we can do to drive that one metric. An example, depending on your business, might be:

New database opt-ins.

Your historical data tells you that for every new database opt-in you get, you are able to schedule X percent new sales appointments. Now, based on your percentage of appointments to transactions, you can predict your sales figures. Based on your average order value, you can now predict your revenue. Based on your average cost of goods and general administrative expenses, you can now predict your profit. Now you have the numbers you need to project cash flow, cash in the bank, and other key metrics. All those metrics are a "downstream" result of the single economic denominator of database opt-ins. Control, measure, monitor, and drive that single economic denominator, and you can control and drive all the key metrics in your business.

All of this can be monitored and measured on a single-view dashboard or piece of paper, no matter how big the enterprise.

THE MASSIVE TRANSFORMATION FORMULA

Okay. Ready to put some of this to work? I thought so. Grab a piece of paper, and let me show you how in a few metrics you can massively transform your business—or any area of your life. I call it my *Massive Transformation Formula*. It has three components:

MTF COMPONENT NUMBER ONE: YOUR BIG 3 GOALS

I don't care if you have a bucket list of 50 things or a thousand places you want to see before you die or a list of 25 goals. As Jim Collins says about priorities, I say about goals—if you have more than three goals, you don't have any. I'm not talking just any three goals. These are the three goals that, if you achieved them, would make this year, undeniably, the best year of your life.

"You are only one or two key habits away from a massive transformation in any area of your life."

Yeah, those kind of goals. Your big, hairy, and audacious goals. Decide what those BIG 3 goals are, and then tear a page out of the Buffett method and throw the rest of the list away. You've already decided what would make this the best year of your life. Everything else will only distract your focus and drain your capacity for making the BIG 3 possible.

MTF COMPONENT NUMBER TWO: KEY HABITS

Once you know *where* you're headed, what do you need to do to get there?

This question is trickier than it looks. Most people think there are a thousand things they have to do to accomplish their big goals. The reality is that you are only one or two key habits away from a massive transformation in any area of your life. Think about it. Take sales, for instance. There are one or two key habits that if repeated, day in and day out, relentlessly and consistently over a long period of time, would massively transform your results. The same is true about health and fitness, your marriage, your parenting, and your leadership. The key is to identify the one or two key habits that are *most important* to the achievement of each of your BIG 3 goals.

Once you have those one, two, or three key habits critical to the achievement of each of your BIG 3, you have everything you need to be successful. Now you just need to do them, over and over again, without fail. That's where number three comes in.

MTF COMPONENT NUMBER THREE: TRACK

You engage in your habits, good and bad, without even knowing it—that's why we call them habits. They happen whether you think about them or not.

Do you remember when you were first learning to drive a car? You were told to keep your hands at ten and two o'clock. Be sure to check the rearview mirror regularly. Check the left mirror, but put the turn indicator on first. Check the right mirror. Use your right foot for the gas and the brake... oh and if you had a stick shift, then your left foot has to do this, along with your right foot and right hand simultaneously. All the while, scan everything you see out the front window and avoid oncoming traffic.

It seemed impossible, right? How can you possibly think of all these things and do all these things simultaneously?

Well, how about now?

Now you can drive down the road while having a conversation with passengers, eating, applying your makeup, shaving, or talking on your cell phone. You don't have to *think* about driving at all. Why? Because it became automatic. It became a learned habit.

You've probably had the experience I have where you've been driving down the freeway, then looked up and suddenly realized you missed your exit several miles ago. This means you've been hurtling your car down the freeway at 70 miles an hour completely brain dead... or at least completely unconscious.

To avoid missing the "exits" on the freeway of success (and that means missed opportunities), we need to turn off autopilot and come back online. We need to bring awareness to our unconscious behaviors, and only tracking will make that happen. When it comes to tracking our BIG 3 goals, every night we need to borrow an idea from the restaurant business and "cash out."

CASH OUT EVERY DAY

From ages thirteen to eighteen, I was a waiter. During a typical shift I'd punch in food and drink orders, serve the customers, and then take payments in the form of credit cards and cash at the end of the meal, plus tips (hopefully!).

At the end of the night, I always had to sit down with the store manager and "cash out." All the credit card receipts plus the collected cash had to match up with the total order amount logged into the computer. Any overage was mine to take home as tips, and if the numbers didn't match up and I came up short, I had to make up the difference myself.

Shouldn't we all have to cash out at the end of the day? These are the behaviors and habits you said you were going to do today. Did you do them? Does your plan match your action? Do your numbers add up? If not, put yourself in trouble!

It takes less than thirty seconds to review your BIG 3 and the half dozen key habits you planned to execute each day. Check off each one: Check! Check! Uh-oh, check! Uh-oh! Uh-oh! Now you'll know if you are on track or off track.

Tracking your habits prevents drift. *You need to know if you're on track.* If you don't know, you can drift. You can wake up overweight, broke, divorced, and wonder how you got there.

You see, we don't fall off course, we *drift* off course. We don't fall off our workout schedule, our diet, our resolutions, our goals—we drift. We drift ever so slightly and slowly without realizing it. Then a while down the road, we finally regain consciousness, only to realize we are completely off course. To prevent this drift you have to be strict about tracking your progress (or lack thereof) every day, all along the way. This is why the essential component of my *Living Your Best Year Ever* program is the Weekly Rhythm Register—a one-page weekly tracking system. That single page is responsible for an untold fortune in income, good health, satisfying relationships, and many other goals and behaviors I've achieved using it.

Believe it or not, you really are just three steps away from massive transformation. Do what other superachievers do and narrow your list down to three big goals that, if reached, would make this the best year of your life. Then identify the key behaviors you need to do each and every day to support those goals, and track your progress each and every day to prevent drift.

4. YOUR VITAL IMPROVEMENTS

Because impact is my vital metric, I do enjoy engaging in conversation with *SUCCESS* fans on my Facebook page. And one day, someone posted this comment:

"You've inspired me to read more. This year I've set a goal to read 32 books."

Of course, I was pleased to have helped someone and clearly they were pleased with their chosen goal…. But something about the comment just didn't sit well with me. I quickly responded:

"I think it'd be better if you read one great book 32 times."

Reading 32 books means you're reading a lot, which is better than watching a lot of TV or other alternatives, but does it mean you're *applying* it? My guess is no. If you're looking to improve, as all of us should, just reading a bunch of books about improvement isn't enough. It takes time, persistence, and deliberate practice in a narrow range of activity to truly improve.

The comment left by a well-meaning would-be achiever revealed something critical about the entrepreneur roller coaster: You don't succeed just by *learning*. You have to *study*, then *do*. We need to learn less and *do* more.

"It's not what you learn or what you know; it's what you *do* with what you learn and know."

@DarrenHardy #JoinTheRide

Do you really need to read another book on how to lose weight? *You already know how.* Do you need another seminar? Another audio program? Knowledge is *not* power. That's a myth. It is the potential for power, but it is not power itself. It's not what you learn or what you know;

it's what you *do* with what you learn and know. There is a significant difference between learning and improving, and the difference is taking action and producing measureable results.

Have you ever been to a seminar, listened to an audio program, or read a book that promised life-transforming results in 90 days or less... and it didn't happen? Yeah, I know. Me, too. We have a tendency to say, oh, that book, that CD, that program, that seminar didn't work. Noooooo, it wasn't the material that didn't work. *You* didn't *do* the work.

When it comes to improving yourself, you need to be as focused and deliberate as you have been throughout this entire chapter. Here is the basic framework for significant improvement that will last:

STEP 1: IDENTIFY

You can't be "Jack of all improvement" or you'll be the master of nothing. You have to narrow your areas of focused improvement. What's the best way to do that? Focus on improving those skills that are the most vital to the achievement of your BIG 3 goals.

As my BIG 3 goals have changed over the years, so have the skills I have focused on improving. When I was in real estate, I studied the art of face-to-face sales. When I started speaking to audiences on a regular basis, I focused entirely on strengthening my presentation skills. Leadership, persuasive writing, time management skills—each quarter I figure out what skill is most needed to advance my BIG 3 goals, and I then attack it. I buy the top five books on the topic, the top three audio or video programs on the topic, and sign up for (at least) one seminar focused on that skill. Then I spend the quarter studying, practicing, and tracking my improvement on that vital skill.

STEP 2: INVEST

At eighteen years old I was told by Brian Tracy that every dollar you invest in your personal development adds thirty to your bottom line.

I was inspired by that idea. I made $150,000 that year, and I took

$15,000 and reinvested it in my personal development. The following year, I grew tremendously, and I've followed his advice ever since. And I'm not the only one. The greatest athletes in the world hire the most expensive coaches, consultants, and advisors. The greatest companies do the same. CEOs and celebrities, too. Why? Because they know that investing in themselves is what got them to where they are, and they know they need to keep doing it to grow and stay at the top of their game. As my mentor Jim Rohn would continually remind me, "If you want to have more, you have to become more. You have to grow into your goals."

Before you fund your 401(k), before you invest in a startup, before you invest in that stock, invest in *yourself*. Where else are you going to get that 3,000 percent return that Brian Tracy is talking about? Not in the stock market. Bet on yourself—it always yields the highest returns.

STEP 3: RINSE AND REPEAT

I'm a big believer in finding someone or something that works for you and going deep with it. I call it the "rinse and repeat" practice. I feel it's better to find a training and development source, resource, or leader that resonates with you. Someone you like and align with philosophically. Then "rinse and repeat" with them over and over.

For instance, I went to Jim Rohn's Leadership Weekend six times. People thought I was crazy (for more than just this, admittedly). They would say, "But you already went. You've heard it all before. Whaddya, slow?" And it's true (not the slow part). Jim did the exact same lecture, told the same stories and the same jokes (I laughed every time!) each of the six times. But mysteriously, I got something totally different each and every time. Certainly it was because *I* was different—I was dealing with different issues and challenges each time, and I was at different levels of my personal growth each time.

Attending the same workshop that I already knew was great, led by someone I already respected and aligned with philosophically, was far better for me than attending six different seminars. Those new events would have done more to perplex my mind than they would have done to

203

ENTREPRENEUR

deepen my understanding of the existing principles of success I already knew to work.

I see people dig too many shallow holes and wonder why they never strike oil. Instead, once you dig a hole that has oil in it (find someone or something you like), keep drilling—go deeper. Mine that well for all it's got. Then rinse and repeat.

In the end, the fundamentals of success are simple and easy—getting yourself to stick to them is the difficult part. Don't make it even more difficult by confusing yourself with too many arbitrary opinions and conflicting ideas.

A SUCCESS VITALS SUMMARY

Your success vitals boil down to one simple concept: Decide on a few critical things, do them more often, then get better at them.

That's it. That's the fundamental secret of extraordinary success. Of greatness. Simpler than you thought? Probably. But not always *easy*.

The fundamentals of your life and your business can be deceptively simple. We know that some of the legendary achievers constantly return to fundamentals over and over again. In part, to make sure they master them, but also to develop the discipline required to stick to them.

"Productivity isn't magic. It's discipline."

@DarrenHardy #JoinTheRide

Productivity isn't magic. It's discipline. It's the discipline that separates the superachievers from everyone else. It's the discipline that delivers the results that compound over time and allow you to control the ride.

As legendary coach Vince Lombardi said, "The key to winning is to be brilliant at the basics."

SO WHAT'S STOPPING YOU?

Many people step on to the entrepreneurial roller coaster so that they can *finally*, after years of working for someone else, not have a boss.

Well guess what? It turns out you do still have a boss. It's *you*.

How good is that boss?

Is your "boss" letting you get away with lack of accountability? With being distracted? With slacking, using lame excuses, and dodging responsibility for the important things?

Maybe you need to boss yourself around a little more.

Are you taking control of yourself? Focusing on what's vital? Because *that's* how you take control of the ride.

ENTREPRENEUR

ACTION PLAN

GO TO THE RESOURCE PAGE AND COMPLETE THE WORKSHEETS ON:

- Understanding and calculating your value

- Identifying your success factors
  - Vital functions
  - Vital priorities
  - Vital metrics
  - Vital improvements

- Formulating your massive transformation

Go to: RollerCoasterBook.com/Resources

The dangers of life are infinite, and among them is safety.

—Johann von Goethe

CHAPTER 7
HANDS IN THE AIR

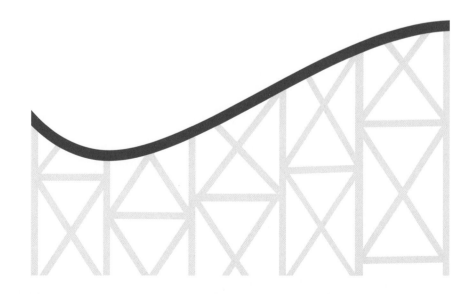

TERROR IS PART OF THE THRILL (NO, REALLY)

I remember my first ride on Space Mountain in Disneyland like it was yesterday. Normally I don't have much of a memory for these kinds of things, but this ride stuck with me.

I didn't like it. At all.

The reason was simple: No one warned me.

I was just making my way through the park, lining up for one ride after another. I had no clue this one would change me—forever.

It was the summer of 1979, and I was eight years old. The park was so hot I thought my Vans were going to melt right off my feet. Space Mountain was jam-packed, and I was trying to cool down in the line outside by eating a blueberry snow cone. It wasn't working. I was cooking as the line slowly snaked its way to the entrance.

At last, I reached the interior of the massive futuristic building, and the hot sun was replaced by black lighting that made my white tank top glow in the near-darkness inside. When we finally reached the "Space Port," I said goodbye to the last of my snow cone and stepped on board my "rocket"—the Disney-fied roller coaster car that would be my spaceship for the next few minutes.

The rocket shuttled from the loading area to mission control, and an attendant checked my lap bar. I flashed my bravest blueberry-stained smile to prove I wasn't scared. And then… nothing. We just sat there, painfully awaiting our turn, while the butterflies—and, to my dismay, the snow cone—started to stir in my stomach.

No problem, I told myself. *I've got this.*

I had just conquered the Matterhorn, after all. This ride wasn't nearly as big. How bad could it be?

I was about to find out.

With a jerk, the rocket was released in a kaleidoscope of red strobe lights. We turned and made a small climb through a tunnel of flashing blue lights, another easy turn, and then more climbing.

It's just another roller coaster, I chanted.

Then the lights went out and all hell broke loose.

The interior of Space Mountain is essentially a hollow, dark shell. Everything is pitch black, except for the thousands upon thousands of stars and comets scattered across the "sky."

I barely had time to marvel at the illusion of being in outer space before my rocket fell into a death drop. I was plastered back into my seat until the wild free fall was broken by a hard right turn, then a yank to the left, each one smashing my head off the backrest.

I was starting to panic. By the wise old age of eight, I considered myself a roller coaster connoisseur, but this was something else entirely. I had no way to brace myself for what was coming next because I couldn't *see* what was coming next! In utter darkness, my rocket plunged into a series of tight right turns, going faster and faster. Right then, I was convinced I was going to die. At eight years old, Darren Hardy, fearless ride master, was about to die screaming in outer space.

Just when things couldn't get worse, I was yanked by a sudden left turn and a drop that sent the butterflies in my stomach into revolt. Half of my snow cone came back up and onto my white tank top. Now I wasn't just going to die, *I was going to die in shame.*

About the time I was wondering if the undertaker would tidy me up before carrying me away, the rocket slid into the re-entry tunnel and braked hard. A light flashed—probably a camera to capture my blueberry-stained embarrassment—and the ride made its final turn into mission control. The music faded.

It was over. I did it. And I was still alive.

211

ENTREPRENEUR

THE THRILL OF A LIFETIME

For me, Space Mountain was—and is—much scarier than any other ride. Unable to see what's ahead, it's impossible to prepare yourself for what comes next. The unexpected turns and drops feel more severe, and the speed feels dangerous, life-threatening even—always plunging into the unknown and facing (seemingly) certain doom.

This, of course, is exactly what it feels like to be an entrepreneur.

A normal roller coaster—like a normal life—can be scary enough. But a ride done in the dark transforms the experience from scary to downright terrifying.

But it's also part of what makes it so awesome.

To this day if I ever find myself at Disneyland, the first thing I do is head up Main Street and cut to the right to ride Space Mountain.

It still scares the bejesus out of me.

And I absolutely love it.

If you become an entrepreneur, you're going to face fear. You're going to be scared. You are going to come face-to-face with daily uncertainty and wonder if your "rocket" is going to derail and if you will die a sudden death. *And* you're going to do all that, in the *dark*, with the added risk of public humiliation if you puke a little on yourself.

Facing those things is nonnegotiable. Once you start, you don't get to choose a ride that won't cause you fear. But you *can* choose to face that fear head on, and, like your own personal Space Mountain, even learn to love it.

In this chapter, I am going to help you do just that.

FACING DOWN FEAR

I was once told the story of a wise elder walking through a graveyard with his young apprentice. The elder proclaimed, "The world's greatest entrepreneur is buried in this cemetery. Can you pick him out?"

After a short search, the young apprentice found the grandest head-stone and pointed to it. "It must be him, right?"

"No," said the elder. "It's the one you are standing on."

The young apprentice looked under his feet. The tombstone was hardly visible and barely marked.

"He lived and died never making more than $30,000 a year," said the elder. "He never had the courage to become an entrepreneur, but had he faced his fears, he would have been the greatest."

Most people never live up to the potential they have been given. The results they produce and the life they experience are only a tiny fraction of what they are truly capable of. Why? What stops us?

Only one thing: fear.

Fear can stifle, block, and bury your potential. Most people who never step up to ride the entrepreneur roller coaster resist because they believe that entrepreneurs are fearless, courageous risk-takers who never doubt themselves.

That couldn't be further from the truth.

Every great entrepreneur starts out scared. Every one. Richard Branson started out scared. Bill Gates started out scared. So did every seemingly heroic figure who makes it to the cover of *SUCCESS*. One hundred percent of them started out scared.

Courage is not the absence of fear—it's feeling the fear and *proceeding anyway*. As Nelson Mandela said, "I learned that courage was not the absence of fear, but the triumph over it. The brave man is not he who does not feel afraid, but he who conquers that fear."

The entrepreneurs who make it are brave not because of the absence of fear, but because they put one foot in front of the other and face down that fear every day.

So how do you do it? It begins with understanding what's really going on when you feel fear.

FEAR IS NOT REAL

Sure, it *feels* real—the pounding heart, knocking knees, and sweaty palms. Those are real enough symptoms, but the thing we're actually afraid of is an illusion, an invention of the mind.

Ultimately, a spider can't make you scared. A prospecting call can't make you scared. The only thing that can make you scared is *how your mind interprets those things.* Fear is a phenomenon that resides entirely within your own brain. It's the *mind* that gives every interpretation meaning—it's your *mind* that conjures the negative emotion.

"Fear is not real. It's an illusion, a phenomenon that resides entirely within your own brain."

@DarrenHardy #JoinTheRide

Fear itself doesn't actually exist.
Fear is not real.

This is why one person can look over the edge of a cliff and be gripped by a fear of heights while another finds great joy in cliff-diving or jumping out of an airplane. The reality is the same, but the mind's interpretation and the emotion it generates are different.

Two people can be looking at the same dog—a German shepherd, let's say—sitting there quietly. One person sees it, interprets threat and danger, and feels fear. The other person sees the dog and interprets affection, tenderness, and protection. Instead of fear, this person feels love. The same dog, but two wildly different interpretations and emotional responses—all generated exclusively by the mind.

Why is this? What's happening?

OUR ANCIENT BRAIN

What we call "modern times" make up the last 6,000 years or so, dating back to the start of recorded history. Six millennia may seem like a long time, but mankind has been around for much, much longer.

For hundreds of thousands of years before that—what we might call "primitive times"—humans were still around but under very different circumstances.

During those primitive years, our brains had to be on constant alert in order to protect us from some serious threats—lions and cougars hidden in the brush, leopards stalking from the trees, even attacks from neighboring tribes. With danger lurking behind every corner, it was the humans with the brains that best monitored and most quickly responded to threats who survived to reproduce. If you were slow on the threat-sensing, you were lunch. The stakes were high, and by necessity, as a species we became *very* good at identifying threats and responding to them.

In today's times we are not under the same sort of constant mortal threat in our day-to-day environment. But much of our primitive brain is still here, operating at full throttle. It's still doing its job, triggering the same nervous system responses to threats. The only problem is now, instead of lions and cougars and leopards, our nervous system has identified something else as a threat.

The fear and flight response signals the brain gave our ancestors when they were face-to-face with a roaring lion are the same signals we now feel when we look at a telephone before making a prospecting call. The fear and panic brain response that was caused when a small warrior tribe attacked our ancient relatives is the very same brain response we feel when standing in front of a small group to give a presentation. The same nervous and alarm signals that the primitive brain gave our ancestors when they stood vulnerable and exposed on an open plain is the very same mechanism that is responsible for how we feel when we stand on stage in front of a large group.

This is why we have disproportionate fear responses to inane modern activities. We're using a primitive tool to run a modern-day life.

And that means it's time to modernize your brain.

ENTREPRENEUR

SIX BRAIN HACKS TO CONQUER FEAR

So your brain has a mind of its own—literally. Unfortunately, you're kind of stuck with the original, outdated equipment. Although you can't change the evolution of your ancient mind, you can short-circuit its primitive tendencies by hacking it.

Here are six brain hacks to bring your brain back from the Stone Age and into the age of high-tech tools and roller coaster businesses.

1. GET REAL

The first thing to do is to gain perspective. You want to separate reality from fantasy. It's not a lion—it's a *phone*. If you dial it and the other person answers, *they can't eat you*. If you stand in front of a small group, they are not going to pillage your village. If you stand alone onstage to give a presentation, the audience is not going to attack you. *You are in no mortal danger.*

A good question to ask yourself before doing anything you *think* you fear is, "If I do this, am I going to die?" If the answer is no, then your fear is made up is grossly overdramatic, and it should have no power over you.

2. IT'S THE FEAR OF FEAR YOU FEAR

Oddly, it's not even calling a stranger or making a speech that generates our fear, it's the *anticipation* of doing it—which is, once again, an illusion of the mind.

In the 1960s, a researcher named Seymour Epstein got curious about skydivers. He fitted novice parachutists with heart rate monitors that measured their pulses as their plane climbed toward the release point. He found that—as you might expect—while still safe inside the plane, a jumper's heart rate got faster and faster as the plane ascended. The higher the plane went, the higher the anxiety.

What he didn't expect to find, however, was that once they threw themselves out the door of the plane and started hurtling toward the Earth with only a few thin cords and a glorified bedsheet to keep them from impending doom, their heart rates *declined* dramatically, and they admitted to quite enjoying themselves.

The most stressful part of the entire experience was the illusion of how frightening the event would be or, in other words, the anticipation of fear. Once the reality of the event took over, the fear vanished.

This "pre-fear" is what happens before you pick up the phone, before you go onstage, and before you walk across the room to introduce yourself to a stranger. It's the *anticipation* of fear kicking in—your ancient mind's illusion. Once you are engaged in the activity, your brain realizes that you are *not* toe-to-toe with a predator and this is *not* the primitive mortal threat you feared it would be, and it turns off the fear response.

Just remember: *The fear itself hurts more than the thing you're scared of.*

"It's the fear of fear you fear. The fear itself hurts more than the thing you are scared of."

@DarrenHardy #JoinTheRide

217

ENTREPRENEUR

3. TWENTY SECONDS OF COURAGE

Courage is overrated. Or at least overestimated. You don't need to be brave all day, every day to be successful.

In fact, you barely have to be courageous *at all*.

According to my calculations, you can be a coward 99.9305556 percent of the time. That's your whole day, except for *just 20 seconds*, three times a day.

Why 20 seconds? Because in just 20 seconds, you can…

… pick up the phone to call that "Big Kahuna" prospect.

… introduce yourself to your dream client at a networking meeting.

… walk up to a circle of strangers and say, "Hi."

... volunteer to come up onstage.

... ask him or her out on a date.

... begin your pitch presentation.

... take a plunge into icy cold water.

... start a tough conversation with a loved one or employee.

... say "no" even though it will make you unpopular.

... even jump out of a plane!

So. What should we do when we hit the inevitable wall of fear?

Do this: Shut off your brain. Close your eyes, hold your breath (if you need to), and do what every signal of your brain is insisting you don't do—RUN RIGHT AT IT!

Think about it. In order to jump out of a plane flying thousands of feet in the air and free fall to the Earth, you have to shut your brain *off*. The brain's only job is survival. There is no way you can intellectually convince the brain that jumping out of a plane is a good idea. It will never allow you to do it. Ever. You have to turn it off for the few seconds you need to hurl your body out the door.

Those 20 seconds of courage are enough time to get engaged in the activity and for your brain to realize it won't get eaten. From there on, it's all easy breezy.

The activities you are most afraid of are the activities that can cause a breakthrough in your success. Think of everything you could accomplish if you forced 20 seconds of bravery on your primitive mind just three times a day? Imagine how doing so would multiply your success, lifestyle, and prominence in the marketplace. Think of the breakthroughs you could create.

And! You could still be a coward 99.9305556 percent of the time—just a really rich and successful one!

"The activities you are most afraid of are the activities that can cause a breakthrough in your success. Step into them."

@DarrenHardy #JoinTheRide

4. FOCUS ON TASKS, NOT OUTCOMES

Your brain is a drama queen. It makes mountains out of molehills. It sees a flea and magnifies it into a Tyrannosaurus rex. I call this the *twisted mind* effect.

A friend of mine recently visited the mall with his wife and fourteen-year-old daughter, Ashley. After some individual shopping, he met with his wife at their agreed-upon meeting spot.

When he asked his wife where Ashley was, she said she thought their daughter was with him, as she had been when they originally parted ways. "She was with me just a few minutes ago," he said, "but she said she was going ahead to meet you. She should be with you."

"I haven't seen her," his wife responded.

They both looked at each other, worried.

After a long two minutes of waiting and scanning every person who walked by, panic set in. The father took off running, retracing every step they had taken in the last hour. The mother asked shoppers she saw if they had seen a girl of her daughter's description. As they both looked frantically for their daughter, visions of abduction and child predators flooded their minds. Within ten minutes, they had three store security guards and a team of four mall cops huddled to begin a full-scale

Ashley-hunt. Mom was crying. Dad was yelling.

Moments later, Ashley bounded up cheerfully to the group with a braces-filled smile, asking, "Hey, what's going on?"

Her mom burst out a yelp, ran up to her, and nearly squeezed the life out of her. Her father, shaky and on the brink of tears himself, joined the family hug. "Where were you?" he asked.

"I was trying on a pair of pants in the store right there," Ashley said, pointing to a shop fifty feet away.

In a span of twelve minutes, the minds of the mother and father magnified the reality of their daughter being just a few minutes tardy into projections of her being abducted, molested, and murdered.

That's the twisted mind effect.

And it happens all the time… and to the best of us.

The solution isn't to ignore important things but instead to focus on the task at hand without magnification. It's not only a better way to get through life, but it's the secret of the great pressurized-playmakers.

When Michael Jordan is about to get the ball to take the winning shot, he isn't thinking about the outcome and how this shot will define the season, the championship, the Sports Center highlight, his career, and legacy. He's only thinking about the shot—one he has taken a million times.

When Tiger Woods is standing over the final putt on the eighteenth green of the Masters on Sunday, he isn't thinking how this one stroke could be the $500,000 difference between victory and second place. He's not thinking of his Majors win competition with Jack Nicklaus, and he's not thinking about the several-million-dollar spike this one putt will generate in his endorsement deals. He is only thinking about the task. That one putt. A stroke he has made a million times.

The same rules apply to you in the moments when anxiety closes in. You, too, can become a pressurized-playmaker. Just focus on the task— picking up the phone, holding your hand out and saying "Hi," looking in the eye of your client and saying, "Sign here." Don't let your mind twist itself into a frantic mess by focusing on the magnified (and usually negative and false) outcome.

5. HABITUATE YOURSELF TO FEAR

One organization that understands better than any other how to beat our innate fear response is the military. If the average person is scared to make a speech, imagine what the average undisciplined and slovenly teenager's response to being *shot at* and attacked by insurgents might be. The military takes these young newbies who've never been far from the bosoms of their mothers, and through the boot camp process, they turn them into fearless warriors.

As part of the transformation, new recruits are subjected to relentless and repeated fear, pressure, and stress. The result? Would-be soldiers are habituated to fear. Now, when they're 8,000 miles away from home in Afghanistan and the bullets start flying, they don't run in the opposite direction.

It takes a well-hacked brain to face enemy fire and run *toward* it. But if you can train your brain to run at bullets and bombs, think how easy it can be to train it to run toward a stage, a prospecting call, or a group of strangers.

This process started for me as a kid under the habituation coaching of my "Gunnery Sergeant" father. During my first game of Little League, I kept jumping out of the batter's box when the pitcher threw the ball. In my defense, it's a normal brain response when a flying orb is coming at your head. But it's not good for hitting a baseball.

Plus, in my dad's opinion, I looked like a sissy.

My dad definitely *was not* going to father any sissy, so the next Saturday he took me to the baseball diamond for some batting practice. This was no Disneyland—I was not excited about this father-son excursion.

"All right," he said, "stand in that box. Your feet never leave that box. I don't care where this ball is—*your feet never leave the box*. You hear me?"

I heard him—but just barely over the sound of my knees knocking.

He started with a whiffle ball, and threw it right at me. I flinched, and it hit me, but the light plastic ball didn't hurt. He kept throwing it at me over and over. The more he threw it, the less I flinched or moved. Then he started throwing it over the plate so I could swing at it. Every once in a while he threw it right at me on purpose, but I was frozen in that box like a statue.

Next, he took out a tennis ball and repeated the process. The tennis ball hurt a little more—just enough to matter. But I got used to seeing the ball come at me over and over until I didn't flinch.

"All right," he said, "now we're gonna use a baseball."

Seeing my face, he added, "Look, I'm not going to *try* to hit you, but if I do, no big deal, okay?"

I was skeptical.

"I'll tell you what," he continued. "If I hit you three times, we'll go to pizza when were done."

Now, I *really* liked pizza back then, so I agreed.

Near the end of the long batting practice, he had only hit me once, and I found myself actually leaning in to the next pitch hoping to shorten the time-gap between me and a piece of pepperoni sausage. "Ha! There's two!" I shouted from the batter's box. "One more and we go to pizza!"

We practiced many times after that, and I always found a way to get hit three times. In fact, I got so used to getting hit with the ball that it became my greatest strength in baseball. I would crowd the plate, just asking to be hit. It drove pitchers crazy. I got on base by *being hit* more than most great hitters do by *getting hits*. But I got on base, baby!

My greatest weakness became my strength because I habituated myself to it. As a result, I no longer feared it. You can do the same with your fears. Do the thing you fear over and over again, until you train your brain that it's no longer something to be feared. Not only will the fear lose all power over you, but that fear can become the very thing that separates your success from everyone else's mediocrity.

6. MAKING FEAR AND FAILURE FUN

I got into real estate when I was only 20 years old. At that point, I had no experience and no knowledge of the business at all. I was starting from scratch and was a complete novice.

At my first real estate seminar, I asked the lecturer to lunch and grilled him for his best tip on being successful in the industry.

"My best tip? Sure. Go fail. *A lot*," he said.

"What?!" I said. "I thought the whole idea of success was to avoid failure."

> # "The key to success is massive failure. Your goal is to out-fail your competition."
>
> @DarrenHardy #JoinTheRide

"Quite the opposite," he said. "The key to success is *massive* failure. Your goal is to out-fail your competition. In most businesses, whoever can fail the most, the fastest, and the biggest wins."

I was still perplexed. As far as I was concerned, failure was something you tried to do as little of as possible.

To clarify, he picked up a cocktail napkin and pulled out a pen. "Life, growth, and achievement," he said, "work like a pendulum." He drew a simple diagram on the napkin. "On one side, you have failure, rejection, defeat, pain, and sadness. On the other side, you have success, acceptance, victory, joy, and happiness. If you stand still in life, you won't experience much failure and pain. But you won't find much success and happiness either.

"Over time," he continued, "most people figure out how to operate in a narrow comfort zone. They can only allow the pendulum to swing a small distance into pain, rejection, and failure, thus they only experience the same small degree of joy, connection, and success on the other side of the swing."

The key is you cannot experience one side without an equal proportion of the other. This is the mistake most people make: They think they can have success without failure, love without heartache, and happiness without sadness. As sure as we have gravity, we have the pendulum swing of success and failure.

He added, "Now you really can't control the side of success. Often

223

ENTREPRENEUR

what you pursue eludes you. But the one side of the pendulum you can control is the side of failure and rejection. That is why it is your job to go swing that pendulum as high and big as you can. Go fail. Big. Fast."

I had nothing to lose, so I just took his advice at face value. I really went for it. I became a failure-seeking maniac. I strategized on how I could get as much failure, as big and as fast as possible. Fortunately, in real estate sales, there are several ways.

One is calling on expired listings. As I mentioned earlier, these are people who had their house on the market with another agent and it didn't sell. The minute the listing shows up as "expired" on the computer, 50-plus agents call immediately. Sellers, unsurprisingly, quickly become mad and confrontational. Oh goody, lots of rejection, pain, and sadness there!

Then there were the FSBOs—"For Sale By Owners." These are people who hate Realtors so much they wouldn't even think of listing with one. There is *plenty* of pain, sadness, defeat, rejection, and failure to be had there, too.

When I was finished with all of them (and done wiping the tears from my eyes!), I would park my car at the end of a street and get out. I carried a little note pad with 50 checkboxes on it, and I wouldn't allow myself to get back in the car until all 50 boxes were checked. Then I'd go knock on doors. This strategy elicited plenty of angry jeers, barking and biting dogs, slammed doors, and kids throwing rocks from across the street. Tons o' fun!

Then, for a final serving of pain pie, I'd go to my office. The hours between 5:00 and 9:00 p.m. were "money time." For four hours straight, I would cold call on the phone. Why that time period? Because that's when people are home and usually having dinner. People love it when you call during dinner! Lots of pain, rejection, and sadness to be had there.

But guess what?

First of all, failure got a lot easier. Rejection no longer stung. I started making a game out of it. It actually became kind of comical.

Then something else happened: *The pendulum started to swing back.*

Some of those expired listings listed with me.

Some of those FSBOs ended up converting and listing with me.

And some of those cold doors and cold calls actually *were* looking to sell and listed with me.

That is how I ended up outselling an office of 44 veteran agents, combined… and dominating the city the next year and the entire county of 3,000 agents the following year. I was willing to be a massive failure, and I ended up loving it. In fact, it became quite addictive because I knew it was the controlling factor in my greater success.

If you want to start your pendulum swinging in wider arcs, you'll need to start experiencing more failure. Think of it this way: Level One growth is recognizing that rejection and failure are not bad. You start walking out of the shadows of your fears.

Level Two is accepting failure as part of the process along your journey. That's where many good salespeople and entrepreneurs are. They don't like it, but they accept it as part of the process.

225

"The most successful person in the room is also the one who has failed the most. Go fail!"

@DarrenHardy #JoinTheRide

But to be great? When you become truly unstoppable and rise *way* above everyone else? That's when you reach Level Three. When you don't just see failure as good or just accept it as part of the process, but when you really *love* it, seek it, celebrate it, and become addicted to pushing yourself to gain more of it. That is when all resistance is removed, and the pendulum has nothing left to do but make gargantuan swings on the side of success, wealth, and happiness.

To this day, if I get to the end of the week or month and I have not failed significantly at something, I am mad at myself. Why? Because I want more success. How do I get it? More failure.

Remember: *The key to success is massive failure.*
Go fail!

TERRIFYINGLY THRILLING!

Do you remember your first roller coaster? Not the entrepreneurial kind, but your first honest-to-goodness rail-gripping, knuckle-whitening amusement park ride?

As a kid, the real badge of honor on a roller coaster wasn't to just ride the ride—any chump could do that—but to be able to put your hands in the air. To *not*, in other words, hang on.

> # "Risk means acting without certainty. It's scary. But it's also what makes the entrepreneur roller coaster so thrilling!"
>
> @DarrenHardy #JoinTheRide

The first time, letting go was a real gut-wrencher. Without the feel of the cold bar in your palms, you had no choice but to rely on the seat belt or safety bar to hold you in. And there were moments where you could feel yourself lift right out of the seat.... But, if you could summon the nerve to do it, to let go, a couple of interesting things happened.

First, you learned to *trust*. If you didn't hang on, you had to believe that the safety systems on the ride *worked*. That the seat belt would keep you in. That the shoulder harness would hold you down. You had to believe, in other words, that the systems would support you.

Second, you found the value of facing your fear. You discovered that when you put your hands in the air, you enjoyed the ride more. It was more thrilling. *When you took the risk, you got more in return.* Putting your hands in the air on the ride was a way of turning fear into something positive. *It made the ride better.*

In the real world, in your real business, risk works the same way. You risk more, you get more. You face your fears, and you profit as a result.

Are you ready to ride with your hands in the air? To face your fear?

Risk is, by definition, doing something without certainty. It's riding in the dark. It's more terrifying, certainly. But that's what makes it so thrilling, so rewarding, and so freaking awesome!

227

ENTREPRENEUR

ACTION PLAN

GO TO THE RESOURCE PAGE AND COMPLETE THE WORKSHEETS ON:

- Identifying and facing down your fears

- Crushing your fears

Go to: RollerCoasterBook.com/Resources

It's never too late to be what you might have been.

—George Eliot

CHAPTER 8
SMILE FOR THE CAMERA

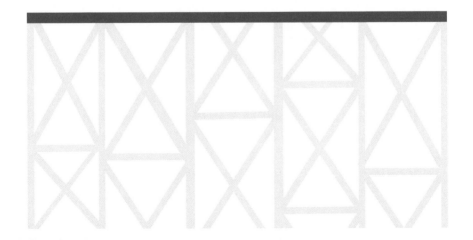

DON'T MISS THE POINT

An Olympic gold medalist and eight-time Grand Slam winner, Andre Agassi is one of the all-time tennis greats. From the age of sixteen, when he turned pro, to the end of his phenomenally successful career, he dominated the sport. He's not just an athlete but a true celebrity as well. If you ranked every sports player in history by lifetime endorsements, Agassi would be fourth in the world.

For all his success, though, Andre seemed incapable of being happy. In fact, not even 24 hours after reaching number one in the world, Agassi found himself roaming the streets, wondering, "What the hell is wrong with me? I'm the number one tennis player on earth, and yet I feel empty."

By 1997, he was more than just empty; he was in trouble. His world ranking dropped, eventually falling to a dismal 141. He was given a drug test and tested positive for crystal meth. He was overcome with depression and a sense of doom. Agassi had become a shadow of the man he once was.

What went wrong? How could this happen? How does a man become wealthy, famous, and number one in the *world* at what he does and still feel empty?

When asked that question, Agassi confessed to a crime many of us have committed:

He simply had the wrong goals.

"I never really wanted to be number one," he said. "That was just something others wanted for me."

Then Agassi found what he wanted. His comeback began when he started a charter school for disadvantaged kids. His own childhood had been dysfunctional, and he had never felt safe. He wanted to create a place where children could feel the security he never enjoyed, a place where kids had a chance at realizing their potential.

Now his achievement on the tennis court meant something new. It was a means to fund his mission—a way to raise millions for a goal he truly believed in. "At last," he wrote in his autobiography, "my fame will have a purpose."

Two years later, Agassi was once again the number one tennis player in the world. He continues to hold the record for being the oldest player to be ranked number one.

There's a key moment on amusement park roller coasters—usually on the fastest, most frightening stretch of track—when you get your picture taken.

When you get off the ride, you'll find groups of people clustered around those photos, pointing, laughing, and commenting on the expressions of people as they pass through the scariest moment of the ride.

Those pictures are an education in themselves. They say a lot about the ride—and the riders. You'll find every expression and body posture you can imagine, from the abject terror of a man trying to crawl beneath the safety bar to hide, to a woman's face-splitting smile of joy as she hits speeds she never thought she'd see, her hair billowing out behind her.

As we wrap up this roller coaster training guide, I want to give you a few of the do's and don'ts of the entrepreneurial ride. I want you to know that no matter when the camera flashes—whether during a skyrocketing ascent or death spiral drop—you'll be smiling.

THE DO'S AND DON'TS OF SUCCESSFUL RIDING

DON'T: WANT WHAT YOU DON'T WANT

In six years and 72 covers, there are only three people we've ever featured twice on the cover of *SUCCESS* magazine. This guy is one of them.

233

ENTREPRENEUR

Why? Because I love the guy.

I *love* Richard Branson.

In fact, I'll let you in on a secret: For years, I wanted to *be* Richard Branson.

I mean, why not? Who *doesn't* want to be a billionaire adventurer playboy with rugged good looks and an apparently inexhaustible supply of enthusiasm? The dude just exudes fun, coolness... and he's a billionaire who has his own private island. How sweet is that?

Yep, Richard was my model of success. I wanted to *be* Richard Branson.

That is, until I got to know him.

Make no mistake, I still love the guy. And he truly *is* cool. But, after studying him, I realized how differently we are wired.

The more I learned about his life, the more I began to realize how miserable I would be if I had to *live* his life. I saw the stress and complexity of heading more than 400 companies. I considered the headaches that come with managing, directly or indirectly, 50,000 employees. And the lawsuits! The inevitable and constant lawsuits! I began to see that although *he* loved it, being Richard Branson would never work for me.

Branson *likes* having 400 plates spinning and doesn't mind if a few fall.

I don't like breaking plates.

I like delivering excellence in a few carefully chosen areas of my life. I've learned this is how I like to live. Fewer things, done excellently, equal happiness for me. Sir Richard Branson, on the other hand, thrives in a very different environment.

Of course, I still find great inspiration and insight in many of his brilliant methods and philosophies, but the greatest lesson he taught me—greater than any growth strategy or innovation technique—was this:

"Don't want what you don't want."

Simple words, with profound meaning.

It's an easy trap to fall into—believe me, I know. It's easy to fall under the spell of someone else's dreams or be seduced by the scorekeeping of other people's goals.

Don't.

> ## "Follow your own path, not the Joneses'. Listen to your own gut, your own heart, not the ambitions of others. Don't let fear, envy, or social pressure cloud your vision."
>
> @DarrenHardy #JoinTheRide

Follow your own path—not the Joneses'. Listen to your own gut, your own heart—not the ambitions of others. Don't let fear, envy, or social pressure cloud your vision. You know what you like and what you don't. You know what fulfills you and what doesn't. Use your intuition, follow the internal pull, and ignore the external distractions.

Chasing someone else's model of success might have you waking up one morning to realize that, like Andre Agassi, you've been chasing something for the wrong reasons.

Don't want what you don't want.

This is *your* ride, after all—no one else's.

DON'T: MISS THE POINT

My dad's mentor was his football coach at Cal State East Bay (then known as Cal State Hayward). My dad called him "Coach" his whole life. Coach grew up in a small farming town in Arkansas as one of nine children. He rose above abject poverty and was my earliest example of a self-made man.

After coaching football, he got into real estate and then became the reason my dad got into real estate (which, in turn, was why I ended up in real estate, as well). He saw business as a dog-eat-dog boxing match, and his financial statement was his scorecard. Over the years, Coach ended up owning several hundred units of real estate and accumulated a staggering fortune.

During one of my visits to the Bay Area, my father asked me to join him to go visit Coach, who, at 70, was in the fight of his life with cancer. By this point Coach could barely lift his head off the pillow. But he could still talk, and for over an hour we laughed and reminisced, telling old stories and revisiting his many accomplishments in life.

When it came time to leave, we said our goodbyes, and I was following my dad out the door when I heard Coach's hoarse voice call out, "Darren! Darren!"

I rushed back over to him, thinking the worst. I put my hands on his hospital bed rails and leaned in.

"What's wrong, Coach?" I asked.

He reached up and grabbed me firmly by the forearm and pulled his head up off the pillow for the first time that day to meet my gaze. He looked at me sternly, and said, "Don't miss the point."

Don't miss the point?

I wasn't sure I understood. What point had I missed? Had there been a point?

He continued, "I had houses. Too many houses. What I needed was more *people*. More *relationships*."

He took a breath.

"I invested money. Money!" he spit out the word. "Heart. I should have been investing my *heart*."

He took another breath. And with this one, I saw his eyes turn a watery-blue. "I was keeping the wrong score, Darren. I was playing the wrong game."

At that moment, the former football coach, the real estate magnate, the man at the very end of his days, released his grip on my arm. He lay his head back on the pillow and, staring blankly at the ceiling, said one last time—to me or himself, I'll never know:

"Don't miss the point."

I swallowed hard. "I won't, Coach. Thank you. I won't."

That was the last time I ever saw Coach. But I'll never forget his words. I live by them now. And I respectfully pass them on to you.

Don't miss the point.

"Don't miss the point. Spend your day pursuing the things you want said in your eulogy."

@DarrenHardy #JoinTheRide

237

ENTREPRENEUR

IS BIGGER BETTER?

Many people follow their ambition with reckless abandon and their ambition comes back to bite them, as it did for Coach.

Before pursuing more for more's sake, pause and ask yourself an important question: *Will being bigger make things better?*

It's a serious question and a very important one to consider. If your knee-jerk response is *yes*, I'd suggest you take the time to be sure. Remind yourself what is most important to you. Is it freedom? Love? Happiness? Health? Connectedness? More time with your children, your spouse, or your friends?

Now ask yourself, will going for bigger bring you more of what you want? If it will, then go for it with everything you've got.

But if it will take you away from the things you want most, then be very careful.

Ambition is a tricky thing. It can power your ride to great speed, and you'll need ambition to drive you to grow, persevere, and realize your capabilities. But it can also drive you off the tracks to your doom. Your ambition will tell you to pursue every shiny object, chase every opportunity, and constantly go for bigger. But it might also drive you right out of your life. Bigger could mean *less* time with family or *less* freedom as you're held prisoner by the demands of your big, big thing.

I'm not afraid to admit that ambition and I have a sordid past. I have learned the hard way that sometimes you fall so desperately in love with the destination that you only realize after it's too late that the journey sucked and the destination wasn't worth it.

START WITH THE END

How do you figure out "the point" so you don't miss it? How do you make sure your ambition doesn't overtake your life, thus leaving you without one? The answer? Start with the end and work backward.

Imagine waking up tomorrow morning, grabbing your cup of coffee, and opening up the newspaper to find *your* obituary announcing your death. That's exactly what happened to Swedish chemist Alfred Nobel in 1888.

Ludvig Nobel, Alfred's brother, had passed away, but a French newspaper mistakenly thought it was Alfred. They printed Alfred's obituary instead.

Alfred was an armaments manufacturer and the inventor of dynamite. For his accomplishments, the premature obituary named him the "merchant of death," holding him responsible for mass destruction and blaming him for the deaths of hundreds of thousands of men.

As Alfred read his own obituary in the paper, he was shocked at the legacy he would one day actually leave behind. He vowed then and there to change it, and in his will, he left the bulk of his enormous fortune to establish the now famous Nobel Prizes. To this day, the Nobel Prizes are the highest awards that can be attained in the fields of literature, medicine, science, economics, chemistry, and peace.

By thinking clearly about the end and the legacy he wanted to leave, Alfred transformed both his present actions and his future legacy.

He, in effect, rewrote his own obituary, and you can do the same. In fact, it's how you can be sure you don't miss the point. Define clearly how you want your obituary to read *now*.

Then start living in alignment with it today.

> ## "Bigger is only better if it's making that smile on your face wider and, brighter and fills the journey with joy. Live today as you want to be remembered in the end."
>
> @DarrenHardy #JoinTheRide

239

ENTREPRENEUR

Remember what Coach said. *Don't miss the point.*

Bigger is only better if it is making that smile on your face wider and brighter and fills the journey with joy. Live today as you want to be remembered in the end.

DO: THE RIGHT THING

I know all too well how difficult it can be to keep your priorities straight when you're constantly presented with ways to make your ride faster or more exciting. With the hot air of ambition breathing down your neck, it's easy to miss the point.

When ambition starts to get the better of me and I'm offered choices that might take my ride into the danger zone, I think of my father and what must have been the most difficult decision of his life.

My parents divorced when I was eighteen months old. My dad insisted on keeping me—something that doesn't happen often now and happened even less in the early '70s. My mother, who never really wanted to be a mother in the first place, cheerfully handed me over.

My dad was only twenty-three and hadn't the faintest idea what to do with a toddler. My grandmother (my other one, my dad's mom), who saw the writing on the wall quite clearly, insisted that he ship me home to live with her. He said no. Undeterred, she got on a plane (for the first time ever) and appeared on our front doorstep one afternoon, insisting he hand me over.

My dad once again refused, which was no small feat. His mother ruled his world. When she insisted, he always relented. Always.

But not this time. This time was different.

My dad told her I was his responsibility and he would do what had to be done. When she pressed him to explain why, he said, simply, "It's the right thing to do."

Shortly after, we moved to Hawaii, where my dad was the football coach for the University of Hawaii. Life was good for my dad then. He had a great job and was doing well. But a year later, his mother died and his father was not handling it well. As my grandfather deteriorated, my dad once again did the right thing. He left his coaching position—a job he *loved*—and moved us back to the Bay Area to live with my grandfather.

Settled in our new situation, my dad now had to look for another job. As I'm sure you can imagine, there are only so many coaching positions available at any given time. Months of searching and applying for positions near my grandfather's home passed. Nothing happened. We were running out of money, and the situation was becoming dire.

Finally a head coaching job opened up at Olympic College in Washington.

Head coach. This was my dad's dream job. It would be the pinnacle of my father's college coaching career, and here he was, so close he could almost taste it. There were three other applicants in the running, and although he was the least qualified, my father hustled, charmed, and gave it his all.

Decision day came on a Friday afternoon. I remember the phone ringing at our house and my father's head turning sharply to stare at it for a moment before he answered. It was the chancellor of the college on the other end of the line, and he had the entire board of 38 people in the room with him. With great excitement and hoopla, they announced that my dad was being awarded the position as the new head football coach of Olympic College.

SMILE FOR THE CAMERA

My father smiled slightly and then replied in a measured tone that he would need to call them back—he needed to talk with his father first. The chancellor, taken aback, agreed and said they would stay and wait in the room together for his return call.

By this time, my grandfather's condition had worsened. Once the most disciplined person I'd ever known, my grandfather had been crushed by the loss of his wife. He had aged a decade in a few short months. His skin was gray, his eyes sunken, and his breath heavy with whiskey all day, every day. He was going to bed with his clothes still on and showing up to work in them the next day, unpressed. When my dad told his father about the job offer in Washington, my grandfather looked away and replied, "I understand. Just do what you have to do, son." The break in his voice gave him away.

My father knew what he had to do.

Five minutes after he was offered his dream job, my dad picked up the phone and called the chancellor. He said, "I have to decline your offer. I have to stay here to take care of my dad."

He hung the phone up and never looked back.

One thing I've always admired about my dad was that he always did the right thing when it mattered. That's no easy task. Sometimes the right choice is a really, really hard one. It might mean doing something that costs you more than you'd like to pay. Sometimes, like for my father, the *right* choice meant *the end*. The end of the dream. The end of that particular ride.

But no matter what, when faced with those choices that are the hardest to make—when your dreams and your ambition and your drive are begging you to do one thing, and your conscience is telling you to do another—think of my father, and remember that the only way you'll have an enduring smile is if you do the right thing.

DO: TRUST YOUR GUT

Once there was a man with a high-paying Wall Street dream job. He lived the high-powered, fast-paced, coveted life of a prosperous New Yorker.

241

ENTREPRENEUR

One day, he was struck with an idea for a business. He already had a great job, so leaving it seemed risky. And certainly, a new business wouldn't offer the perks of his current position.

But there was a problem: The idea just wouldn't go away. Something about it stuck with him—he had a feeling he just needed to try.

The man told his boss at the firm about his risky startup idea. His boss, likely not wanting to lose a high-performing member of his firm, asked the man to take a walk with him through Central Park.

For the next two hours, at the leisurely pace only allowed to the most successful New Yorkers, his boss did everything he could to talk some sense into the man. He explained that if he left, he would be walking away from his sizeable annual bonus for that year. He said the man would be jeopardizing his reputation. He'd be putting his wealth at risk.

The boss's final argument, the one that was certain to persuade an intelligent man about to make the biggest mistake of his life, was that while he thought an online bookstore was a "good idea," it was a better idea for someone who didn't already have a good job.

"Jeff," he said. "Please. Just think about it for 48 hours before making a final decision."

So Jeff thought about it.

He asked himself if, when he was eighty years old, would he regret trying? No. He wouldn't regret trying. He asked himself if he would regret if he failed? No. He wouldn't regret failing.

In fact, the only thing he was certain he would regret was *not* trying. Not trying would haunt him every day.

"When I thought about it that way," he would say later, "it was an incredibly easy decision."

So Jeff Bezos ignored his boss's advice and pleas, left the security of his job on Wall Street, and started his online bookstore—the risky endeavor we now know as Amazon.

What would the world be like if Bezos had listened to his boss, if he hadn't had the courage to ignore the naysayers, to believe in himself, and to step into entrepreneurialism?

Think about it this way: What will the world be like if you listen to the people around you, if you don't have the courage to ignore the naysayers, to believe in yourself, and to step into the car of the entrepreneur roller coaster?

NO REGRETS

Jeff Bezos was wise to work through his decision using a framework to minimize regret because, at the end of our days, that's what we'll be thinking about.

Karl Pillemer, a professor at Cornell University, interviewed more than a thousand older Americans from different economic, educational, and occupational backgrounds and asked them to share the most valuable lessons they'd learned. Overwhelmingly, the focus wasn't on what they did, but what they *didn't* do. Of a thousand people in the later stages of life, what dominated their advice on the lessons of life was *regret*.

One man in his late eighties was asked: "If you could come back and live the life of anyone, who would you want to come back as?"

His answer:

"I would want to come back as the man I could have been, but never was."

"Be the person you 'could have been' now."

@DarrenHardy #JoinTheRide

Wow. Don't wait until you're eighty and filled with regret. Be the person you "could have been" *now*.

243

ENTREPRENEUR

DO: KEEP YOUR RESOLVE

There will come a time, if it hasn't arrived already, when you will start to talk to others about your desire to hop on the entrepreneurial roller coaster—to climb this new mountain of yours.

With great enthusiasm you'll tell them about your business idea. You'll tell them about your dreams, your passion, and your hope for a bigger, brighter future.

These people—your friends, your family, people you love and respect—will listen. They'll nod their heads and grunt small approvals from time to time. But as the conversation goes on, you might notice them fidget or shift in their seats.

They're waiting for you to finish so they can say something like, "What? Are you crazy? You don't know how to climb mountains! What are you thinking?"

When you try to explain why you need to climb the mountains, they'll say, "Look, I care about you. That is just too dangerous. You shouldn't do that. You should just stick to your job. You are lucky to even *have* a job in this economy. Leave the mountains to someone else."

Their words will sting. And for a moment, you may even think they're right—after all, these are the people who know you best.

"Approach your goals like this: 'This is my mountain, and I'm going all the way to the top! You are going to see me either waving from the summit or lying dead on the side. I am not coming back!'"

@DarrenHardy #JoinTheRide

In that moment you are going to have to look them in the eye and say with complete conviction:

No. This is my mountain, and I'm going all the way to the top!

With their criticisms still ringing in your ears, you'll start climbing this mountain. Then others—more friends, other family members, parents at your kid's soccer game, people at the country club—will comment. "You know," they'll say, "I heard that mountain is covered in rough terrain, and the weather is unpredictable. I've had friends who tried to climb a mountain like that before, and they fell off and were badly hurt. Their whole family suffered. They lost their home. They only have one car. It's really bad. Look, I care about you. It's best to just be safe and get off that mountain."

In that moment, you're going to have to look them in the eye and say with complete conviction:

No. This is my mountain, and I'm going all the way to the top!

As you continue climbing your mountain, still more people—so-called "friends" and people you barely know—will say, "Wow. You've been climbing that mountain for a while now, haven't you? It doesn't look like you've gotten very far. How long are you going to keep at it? Do you ever wish you hadn't started?"

And in that moment, as cracked as your fingers are, as heavy as your legs feel, you are going to have to look them in the eye and say:

"THIS IS MY MOUNTAIN, AND I'M GOING ALL THE WAY TO THE TOP. YOU ARE GOING TO SEE ME EITHER WAVING FROM THE SUMMIT OR LYING DEAD ON THE SIDE. I AM NOT COMING BACK!"

But all those comments? The skepticism? The loaded questions? They're not the worst part. No, the eeriest feeling is when they stop asking altogether. When you are just a few weeks or even days from reaching the peak and there is a strange *quiet.*

Because at that point, the mountain-haters have moved on to someone else. They're not even paying attention to you anymore.

You're too far gone.

Now it's just you. You, your resolve, and the crisp mountain air.
And the top is within your grasp.

Keep your resolve. Don't give up. Many entrepreneurs fail not because of their idea, their skill, or the market, but because they give up just when the summit is within reach.

Keep your resolve.
Push on.
And when you reach the top and you take in that incredible view, know that I will be there with you, camera in hand, just waiting to capture that *smile*.

DON'T: FORGET WHY

Business will change you.

You can't ride the entrepreneur roller coaster and stay the same. That person who waits nervously at the ticket booth is never the same when he or she steps off the ride at the other end.

You'll become smarter. More resilient. You'll discover more confidence and build new skills. You'll find that you can do things with ease that you never thought you could do *at all*.

Yes, business will change you. For the better.

But don't forget who you are right now.
Don't forget who you were the day you decided to ride the entrepreneur roller coaster.
Don't forget the dream you had and the excitement you felt.
Don't forget the day you stepped up to the tracks.

Most important of all, don't forget *why*.
Because if you wait until the ride is over to smile, you won't just have missed a great photo op.

You'll have missed the point altogether.

Getting to the end of the ride is not the point. Being a successful rider isn't the point either.

The point is enjoying the ride.

The point is riding for the sheer joy of it.

DO: SEEK YOUR GREATNESS

It was Jim Rohn who taught me the real point and purpose of life. He said, "The goal of this grand human adventure is productivity, pursuing the full development of all your potential. To see all that you can become with all you've been given."

You have been given great gifts. You are capable of awe-inspiring achievement and significant contribution to the people and world around you. You have a responsibility to use the potential you've been given, to apply it and grow it. Jim also warned: "Potential underutilized leads to pain."

What I know for sure is that all you have achieved thus far is only a fraction of your real potential. Your current results are well below what you are truly capable of.

It's time to step up.

Consider this book your clarion call. The call to begin your grand adventure.

It's time to start living the life you were designed for, the life you were meant to live.

It doesn't matter what's happened in the past or where you are starting now. Start right where you are. Start right now.

Decide now to step into your greatness and live as the powerful, courageous, bold, and audacious achiever you are.

Greatness is already inside you. You just need to release it and live in it, fully, every day.

You can. Starting. Right. Now.

ACTION PLAN

GO TO THE RESOURCE PAGE AND COMPLETE THE WORKSHEETS ON:

- Identifying your point

- Starting with the end
  - Template for thinking through and writing your own obituary

- Identifying your regrets (now)

Go to: RollerCoasterBook.com/Resources

Giving is better than receiving because giving starts the receiving process.

—Jim Rohn

EPILOGUE

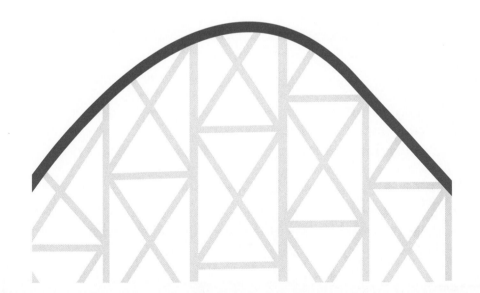

everal months ago, an old childhood friend of mine from the Bay Area was in town on business and asked if I was available to grab breakfast. Mike wanted to catch up, but he also needed some advice. He was thinking of leaving his longtime corporate job and starting a mobile app design company. He wondered if I had any insights, concerns, or even book recommendations as he started this new (and slightly terrifying) journey.

We agreed to meet at my favorite beachside café where the dining room walls are all windows and the view is all ocean. There, we would watch the waves roll in while discussing his plans for his tech world domination.

In preparation for Mike's arrival, I began scanning through my home office library of business books (and trust me, I have a lot of them). I've always found value in these texts—a pearl here, a quote there. They're part of what has helped me become the businessman I am today, and I've always enjoyed gifting them to those who need them.

But on this day, standing in front of my shelves, I was struggling a little.

None of the books were right for Mike.

None of them addressed the exact crossroads at which he stood.

What's going on here? I thought. *What am I missing?*

Surely, *one* of these books had to be appropriate. I ran my finger over every single binding on my bookshelf to make sure I hadn't missed one.

One book talked about leadership but ignored the fact that modern leadership has fundamentally changed.

One discussed start-up strategies but completely left out assessing whether or not you have the emotional fortitude to do it.

One talked about sales techniques that were so old I wondered if they simply redesigned the cover of a textbook from the early 1900s.

The most glaring omission was that none of them would give Mike the three things he needed most: First, a *warning* about the emotional ups and downs he would surely face. Second, the essential *skills* that would make the difference between success and failure. And finally, a powerful *belief* in himself and his capability to pull it off.

Refusing to give up, I began to pull books off the shelf and drop them to the floor. No. No. No. No. *None* of them were going to tell my friend Mike what he *really* needed to know. Not a single book would properly prepare him for the wildest emotional ride of his life.

The following Saturday morning, I sat down with my old friend. Over coffee (him) and a Mango Madness smoothie (me—don't judge) we caught up on old times until the conversation shifted to Mike's big move—becoming an entrepreneur.

"Tell me what I need to know. What conferences should I go to, what videos should I watch, what books should I get?" He was focused and determined.

"Yeah. About that… " I hesitated. It was obvious I had come to our meeting empty handed.

"Or…" He butted in, sensing my awkwardness, "How 'bout you just tell me how you got started?" he said.

And so I did.

I told him about flooding my grandparents' home—how embarrassed I was and how hard it was to pick myself up, squeegee myself off, and keep selling. I told him about the lady who considered investing the last of her savings into starting a business with me—a business I knew wasn't right for her—and how when she asked for my guidance, my integrity caused me to not only turn her away, but also to walk away from a fortune myself. I told him about my conversation with Maria Shriver and the time I got escorted out of Nordstrom. I told him about buying

253

ENTREPRENEUR

my dream home and how badly it hurt when all my father noticed was the tiny water stain in the corner of the ceiling. I told him what Coach told me the last time I ever saw him and even about my blueberry-snow-cone-stained-tank-top coaster ride. I told him about the many, many, many mentors who helped, pushed, and encouraged me as I went. I told him everything.

There we sat, and over the background roar of the ocean, I shared stories I had never really told anyone before. The good, the bad, and the really ugly. Not just the typical "best leadership skills" or "strategic start-up tactics," but the real-life ups and downs, the emotional highs, and the crushing lows.

Mike laughed and nodded, and even scribbled a few notes. But after a while, he became quiet. He looked down, stirred his coffee slowly, and finally asked the question that haunts the mind of every would-be entrepreneur:

"Do you really think I have what it takes?"

I looked at my friend Mike. He wore an expression that I recognized—his eyes were simultaneously scared and hopeful, the corners of his mouth twitched slightly, like they couldn't decide if they should smile or scream.

It was the face of a man standing at the entrance of the biggest, grandest, scariest roller coaster he's ever seen, wondering if he should try the ride.

So I told Mike the only thing left he needed to know:
"I believe in you."

That Saturday-morning breakfast turned into lunch and before we knew it, it was almost happy hour when Mike finally let out a sigh.

"Man. I just wish I would've recorded this or something. I know a few guys who could use this dose of perspective. And even more, they need someone to say to them what you just said to me.... " He stopped as an unexpected lump got caught in his throat.

And that's when I knew.

That's when I knew this book had to be written.

I BELIEVE IN YOU.

I know that inside everyone is a great entrepreneur. I know we're all entrepreneurs at heart—it's in our spirit, our heart, and our dreams. It's in our *blood*. But I also know that running a business is a scary prospect. So scary, in fact, that millions of people are too frightened to even try. And for those who do? It's *hard*. Without help, training, and guidance, a lot of people don't make it—I know I wouldn't have.

Every entrepreneur needs to know that someone believes in him or her, and I will be forever indebted to those who believed in me and shared the insights that empowered my success. The only way I know to pay down that debt is to pay it forward—to tell the whole story, to let you know that the crazy ups and downs you're experiencing (or will experience) are *normal,* and that you have what it takes. That's the main reason I labored to write this book.

If there is one last thing you need before you get on this ride, it's to know that someone believes in you. That someone knows you can do it. And trust me when I say,

I do.

I, Darren Hardy, believe in *you.*

You can do this.

Even if we've never actually met, even if I never get the chance to hear your story, if you've read this far, then know this: *You have what it takes.*

You wouldn't have gotten this far otherwise. Like many books before, you'd have put it down or never found it in your hands to begin with. It's no accident you are reading these words right now. They were written for you.

You were meant to take this ride.

All I ask of you… is to pay it forward, too.

Now. Today.

Who do you know that needs help?

Who do you know that needs to find their entrepreneurial spirit?

Who do you know that needs their business confidence boosted or skills strengthened?

Who do you know that needs this book so he or she can handle the ups and downs of this incredible ride?

Who do you believe in?

We all know someone. The family member who always dreamed of starting something of his own. The friend who's struggling with a business. The colleague who's been punching the clock, too afraid to make the leap and follow his dreams.

Some of them are standing nervously just outside the entrance of the roller coaster, wondering if they can handle the ride.

Some are standing at the ticket booth and need just a last bit of encouragement.

Some are climbing, slowly, toward the first summit and starting to feel the panic.

And some are in the death drop and heading toward the corkscrew, wondering if they are going to survive.

They all share one thing: *They need help and someone to believe in them.*

That someone is *us.*

Together, we can be the ones to help and believe in them.

I believe this book is an essential missing piece for entrepreneurs, and I need your help to reach more of them—to inspire those who haven't yet begun, and help those who have.

Help empower the entrepreneurial confidence, hope, and dreams of just a few other people, and the one who will become most empowered will be *you*. For, as Gandhi said, "The fragrance always remains on the hand that gives the rose."

Thank you for your time, your trust, and your help.
Thank you for believing.

I wish you great success!

—Darren

Knowing is not enough; we must apply. Willing is not enough; we must do.

—Johann von Goethe

FINAL WORD

Congratulations! You have reached a milestone that 80 percent[1] of those around you don't—buying a book and *finishing* it.

But I warn you: Knowledge is *not* power. It's potential power. It's like the energy in a light switch. Until you turn it on to take action, the power is worthless. As Jim Rohn put it to me, "Don't let your learning lead to knowledge, or you'll become a fool. Let your learning lead to action, and you can become wealthy. There's nothing more pitiful than a guy who is smart and broke."

To help you convert your new knowledge into results, here is a final summary action plan:

1) Hopefully, you did as I suggested at the start and treated this book like a workbook, underlining or highlighting the ideas you liked the most. Now pull every key idea *out* of the book and place each one on a 4x6 note card. Write the idea on the front and any explanation needed on the back.

How many did you get? 5, 10, 25, 50, or more?

---

[1] 80 percent of U.S. families did not buy or read a book last year. 57 percent of new books are not read to completion. —According to Statista

2) Lay all your cards on a table or desk and prioritize them based on the potential positive impact each can have on your future and bottom line. Identify at least 10 to 20 of your top ideas.

3) Of those, choose your top three ideas and list a single-step action you can take on each one *now*, such as schedule a planning session, make a call, organize a meeting, or delegate a task. Something to get started and break inertia. All you really need from any book, seminar, or program is three great ideas. Even just one can change your life.

When (and only when) you have fully implemented those three ideas, reshuffle your idea deck and pick your next three top-priority ideas. Now take action on them.

4) Re-read this book at least a half-dozen times. Better yet, I highly suggest you get the audiobook so you can listen to it over and over while you drive, exercise, walk the dog, or cook. Six times—make it your goal.

It's better to "rinse and repeat" one great book several times to ensure you get the most out of it than to move on to your next book or learning program and flush out all the good knowledge you gained from the previous one. You'll be surprised what you see or hear each time you go through a favorite book or program and how it will be exactly what you need in that moment.

5) Complete the exercises at *RollerCoasterBook.com/Resources.* This book provides explanation and motivation, but the real return comes from completing the worksheets I designed for you after each chapter.

6) Register for *DarrenDaily.com* (it's free), where I can provide you daily success mentorship. In under five minutes each workday, I deliver a specially created video, audio, success tip, or insight that you can consume with your morning coffee, tea, or smoothie to help jump-start your day.

Connect with me here:
Blog: *DarrenHardy.com/Blog*
Facebook: *DarrenHardy.com/Facebook*
Twitter: *DarrenHardy.com/Twitter*
LinkedIn: *DarrenHardy.com/LinkedIn*
Instagram: *DarrenHardy.com/Instagram*

That's it. Six steps. I urge you not to skip them.

If I can offer one piece of final advice, it's this: *The success of your business will be found in what you choose to DO every day.*

As a child of the '80s, I particularly like the way entrepreneur and founder of Atari and Chuck E. Cheese's Pizza Time Theaters chain Nolan Bushnell said it:

"The critical ingredient is getting off your butt and doing something. It's as simple as that. A lot of people have ideas, but there are few who decide to do something about them now. Not tomorrow. Not next week. But today. The true entrepreneur is a doer, not a dreamer."

Now is the time to decide. Are you just a dreamer or a doer?

261

ENTREPRENEUR

ADDITIONAL RESOURCES

THE ENTREPRENEUR ROLLER COASTER AUDIO PROGRAM

A vital companion to the book, deepen your learning by listening to the audio program over and over while you are mobile. Darren encourages you to listen at least a half-dozen times. Each time will crystallize an important idea you'll need to thrive on your wild ride.

RollerCoasterBook.com

E-FASTPASS

The Entrepreneur FASTPASS is the essential training system to thrive as an entrepreneur. In this all-in-one, 12-module, digitally delivered intensive training, Darren serves as your personal mentor through mastering the mind-set critical skills you'll need to succeed. This is a game-changing program for all aspiring, budding, or veteran entrepreneurs and business builders.

eFASTPASS.com

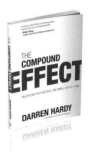

THE COMPOUND EFFECT—JUMPSTART YOUR INCOME, YOUR LIFE, YOUR SUCCESS

This is Darren's popular *New York Times* best-selling book. It is a distillation of the fundamental principles that have guided the most phenomenal achievements in business, relationships, and beyond. It is recommended to get both the book and the audio program.

TheCompoundEffect.com

LIVING YOUR BEST YEAR EVER—A PROVEN SYSTEM TO ACHIEVE BIG GOALS

This is the specific system Darren Hardy developed for himself to design, execute, stick to, and achieve big goals; includes an audio companion.

DarrenHardy.com/BestYear

INSANE PRODUCTIVITY

This is Darren's highly sought-after 12-week training course (with lifetime access) on learning to achieve extreme productivity. Unleash your most productive and powerful self when you learn the productivity system, tools, and strategies used by the most elite achievers of our time, delivered directly to your digital device.

InsaneProductivity.com

HIGH-PERFORMANCE FORUM

An invitation-only private forum led personally by Darren Hardy for CEOs and business leaders committed to building high-growth, high-impact, and high-performing companies.

High-PerformanceForum.com

DARRENDAILY

Darren's (free) daily mentoring. Have coffee (or tea) with Darren every morning where in less than five minutes he will help you kick-start your day and multiply your successes through small, consistent daily improvements.

DarrenDaily.com

NOTES